Questions on Theory of Catering

Ronald Kinton
Garnett College, College of Education (Technical)

Victor Ceserani MBE
Formerly Head of The School of Hotelkeeping and Catering Ealing College of Higher Education.

Second edition

Edward Arnold

© Ronald Kinton and Victor Ceserani 1984

First published in Great Britain 1978 by
Edward Arnold (Publishers) Ltd
41 Bedford Square
London WC1B 3DQ

Edward Arnold (Australia) Pty Ltd
80 Waverley Road
Caulfield East
Victoria 3145
Australia

Edward Arnold
300 North Charles Street
Baltimore
Maryland 21201
USA

Reprinted 1979, 1981, 1982
Second edition 1984

British Library Cataloguing in Publication Data

Kinton, Ronald
    Questions on theory of catering. — 2nd ed.
    1. Caterers and catering — Problems,
    exercises, etc.
    I. Title   II. Ceserani, Victor
    642'.4'076   TX943

    ISBN 0-7131-7303-3

Text set in 9/11 pt English Times
by Colset Private Ltd
Printed and bound by Spottiswoode Ballantyne Ltd,
Colchester, and London

TX
943
,K526
1984

Contents

Introduction

The aim of this workbook is to assist catering students in their revision by providing questions drawn from the 5th edition of *Theory of Catering*. Students may work from the book on their own to test the effectiveness of their study of *Theory of Catering*, and their own general knowledge of the subject. The questions should be answered from memory, from the students' own deductions or by reference to *Theory of Catering*. It is the authors' opinion that revision by systematic use of this book throughout the course will result in a better knowledge of catering.

Many multiple choice questions are included and the book will be particularly useful for students taking City & Guilds of London Catering examinations 705, 706/1 and 706/2, also the Business and Technician Education Council (BTEC) courses and the examinations of the HCIMA.

At the top of each page of questions are the numbers of the pages in Theory of Catering (5th edition) where the answers may be found.

1   Health and safety

pages 1-5

1   Briefly state the two aims of the Health and Safety at Work Act.

1

2

2   At work every employee must take reasonable care of himself or herself and who else?

3   Regarding safety at work, an employee must not interfere with what?

4   An employee should at all times cooperate with whom?

5   Whose function is it to improve the existing standards of hygiene, to act as an adviser and to enforce the hygiene laws?

6   State three ways in which accidents can be caused in the kitchen

1   2   3

7   During a busy kitchen service, the golden rule is 'never run'. true/false?

8   Why may a blunt knife be more likely to cause an accident than a sharp one?

9   State five safety rules to be observed when handling knives.

1
2
3
4
5

10   What is the most important safety precaution to observe when cleaning a cutting machine?

11 Why should guards be in place when using machines?
   ☐ To do the work more quickly.
   ☐ To prevent the operator being injured.
   ☐ To deter stealing.
   ☐ To stop food being spilled.

12 Why should frozen meat be thawed before being boned?

13 If you cut your hand with with a fish bone it may turn s_____

14 A burn is caused by

15 A scald is caused by

16 When an accident occurs who must be informed?
   ☐ the Police   ☐ the employer
   ☐ the hospital   ☐ the health officer

17 The sensible length to wear an apron in the kitchen is
   ☐ ankle length
   ☐ just below the crutch
   ☐ just below the knees
   ☐ under the arms and around the waist

18 When working over the stove it is sensible to have the jacket/overall sleeves rolled up or down?

19 Tick the essential points for an oven cloth.
   ☐ wet   ☐ thin   ☐ torn
   ☐ thick   ☐ dry   ☐ with holes

20 When shallow frying, in which direction is the food put into the pan and why?

21 If foods are tipped out of the frying basket into the friture, a_____must be at hand.

22 To mark the handle or lid or a HOT pan you would
   ☐ write on it the word hot in flour
   ☐ place a piece of red paper on it
   ☐ put the burn ointment beside it
   ☐ sprinkle a little flour on it

23 The correct amount of fat in a movable friture for safety purposes is
   ☐ 2/3 full   ☐ 1/2 full   ☐ 1/4 full   ☐ 3/4 full

24 Wet foods should be d_____ and d_____ before being placed in hot fat.

6

25 Should the fat in a movable friture bubble over on to a gas stove, you
would first
☐ call your immediate superior
☐ call the kitchen porter
☐ lift out the food with a spider
☐ turn off the gas tap

26 When using a mixing machine with a blade, whisk or hook, what is the
essential safety precaution that you should observe?

27 State five safety rules to be observed when using machinery.
1   3   5
2   4

28 A gas explosion can be caused in the kitchen because
☐ there is no pilot.
☐ the gas is turned off at the main.
☐ the main jet has not ignited from the pilot.
☐ the gas has not been turned on.

29 It is not necessary to mop up water spilt on to a kitchen floor as the
heat of the kitchen will do this fairly quickly.
true/false?

30 Why should containers containing liquid never be put above eye-level?
☐ Because other persons are not aware that they contain liquid.
☐ Liquid above eye-level is difficult to control.
☐ Containers above eye-level are heavier.
☐ Liquid in the container moves more when above eye-level.

31 State four signs indicating that a person is suffering from shock.
1
2
3
4

32 What is the first-aid treatment for a cut?
☐ Sprinkle it with salt in order to disinfect it.
☐ Give a glass of brandy.
☐ Wash the skin around the cut and apply a waterproof dressing.
☐ Wrap it in a tea-towel and send for the doctor.

33 If breathing has stopped, a_____ r_____ must be
started before any other treatment is given.

34 Slight burns or scalds should be immersed in
☐ iced water.   ☐ hot running water.
☐ warm water.   ☐ cold running water.

35 In cases of electric shock, firstly
☐ give the person a glass of water.
☐ switch off the current.
☐ apply artificial respiration.
☐ send for a doctor.

30 State three signs which may indicate a person is about to faint.

1   2   3

31 Name two common causes of fire in a catering establishment.

1   2

32 Indicate the correct procedures in the event of a fire in the kitchen.

 Turn off gas and electricity.

 Close doors and windows.

 Run out of the kitchen.

 Turn off fans.

 Warn people in the vicinity of the fire.

 Shout in a loud voice 'Fire, don't panic!'

 Use appropriate extinguishers

 Call fire brigade.

33 If a fire is spreading in the kitchen, what should be done to doors and windows?

34 Match the appropriate extinguisher with the type of fire.

 1 Fire blanket   2 Foam   3 Dry powder

Fire caused by fat	
Electrical fire	
Person's clothing on fire	

35 Complete this fire triangle with one word.

36 To remove the fuel is to _____ the fire.

 To remove the air is to _____ the fire.

 To remove the heat is to _____ the fire.

37 Match these colours to types of fire extinguishers:

blue _____   black _____

red _____   cream _____

green _____

38 What do you understand by a good mise-en-place?

39 Place the following in order to show an efficient flow of work when making croquette potatoes.

Breadcrumbs   Egg wash   Flour   Duchess potato mixture

40   Why is it desirable to have a planned layout when working?

41   Which is the best working method for a right-handed person?

A   B   C

2   Hygiene

1   S_____respect is necessary in every food handler because

2   Personal cleanliness is essential to prevent g_____ getting on to food.

3   Give another word for germs.

4   Hands must be thoroughly washed frequently, particularly

5   Why is jewellery not worn in the kitchen?

6   Which of the following statements is correct?
When handling food you should use
fresh coloured nail varnish.
pink nail varnish.
no nail varnish.

7   Why should finger nails be kept short when handling food?

8 List the faults in personal hygiene shown below.

9 When handling food, hair should be covered
☐ because of the appearance of the worker.
☐ because of the legal requirements.
☐ to keep the customers happy.
☐ because of hygienic reasons.

10 Why are paper handkerchiefs or tissues preferable to linen or cotton handkerchiefs?

11 Why is it important not to sneeze over people, food or working surfaces?

12 Sound teeth are essential to good health.
true/false?

13 You should visit the dentist
☐ every 5 years.
☐ every 3 years.
☐ every 3 - 6 months.
☐ when you have toothache.

14 When tasting food which should you use?
☐ Wooden spoon
☐ Teaspoon
☐ Your finger
☐ Ladle

15 Indicate with arrows where bacteria will be found in large numbers.

16 Cuts, burns, scratches and similar openings of the skin are best covered with
☐ clean gauze.
☐ clean bandage.
☐ waterproof dressing.
☐ antiseptic ointment.

17 Explain two ways in which germs may be transferred on to food by someone smoking in the kitchen.

18 Spitting is an objectionable habit which should never occur, but why is this?

19 Where should outdoor clothing, and other clothing which has been taken off before wearing whites, be kept?

20 What is wrong with this picture of a food handler regarding safety and hygiene?

1   2   3

21 List four essential points to ensure good health and physical fitness.

1   3

2   4

22 When working in a hot kitchen and perspiring freely, the ideal way to replace liquid lost is by

☐ taking salt tablets.   ☐ taking glucose tablets.

☐ drinking pure water.   ☐ drinking beer.

23 Why should picking of food be discouraged?

24 Match the following important points for kitchen clothing:-

1 Protective	to be comfortable in a hot atmosphere	☐
2 Washable	to enable perspiration to be soaked up	☐
3 Suitable colour	need to withstand hard wear	☐
4 Lightweight	so as to indicate the need to be washed	☐
5 Strong	because of the need for frequent change	☐
6 Absorbent	to prevent excessive heat affecting the body	☐

12

25 List the errors you note in this illustration of a cook in the kitchen.

26 To which three groups of people is kitchen hygiene particularly important?

1   2   3

27 Windows in the kitchen used for ventilation should be screened to prevent the entry of dust, insects and birds. true/false?

28 The most suitable surface for kitchen floors is

☐ rubber tiles.   ☐ lino tiles.

☐ quarry tiles.   ☐ concrete.

29 State five important factors of kitchen wall surfaces.

1   2   3   4   5

30 Name three items of kitchen equipment which are difficult to clean and state how you would clean them.

1

2

3

31 When cleaning large equipment such as electrical mixers, slicers etc., what should be done first?

32 Failure to maintain equipment and utensils hygienically and in good repair may cause food _____

33 Why should you not wash aluminium saucepans in water containing soda?

13

34   Why should tinned lined saucepans be dried after being washed?

35   Hygiene is the study of h _____ and the prevention of
d_____ .

36   Number in order of importance
        Having the right attitude to hygiene   ☐
        Seeing films on hygiene   ☐
        Reading books on hygiene   ☐
        Practising hygienic habits   ☐
        Attending lectures on hygiene   ☐

37   Food handlers should not only know the Food Hygiene Regulations,
but should practise them in their daily work. true/false?

38   In a catering establishment can any of the following be excused in
relation to hygiene? Neglect, ignorance, thoughtlessness, low
standards, poor facilities. yes/no

39   The average number of notified cases of food poisoning each year over
the past ten years has been
    ☐ 400   ☐ 8000
    ☐ 4000   ☐ 14000

40   What is food poisoning?

41   List eight ways to prevent food poisoning.

42   By far the greatest number of cases of food poisoning are caused by
harmful _____

43   Food contaminated by _____ is by far the most common
cause of food poisoning.

44   What have the following in common?
    Zinc   Rhubard leaves   Lead   Arsenic

45   By what means can chemical food poisoning be avoided?

46   What word means the same as poisons? _____

47   Bacteria which forms spores can withstand h_____for long
p_____of t_____ .

14

48 Because bacteria multiply by dividing in two under suitable conditions, one bacterium could multiply in 10-12 hours to between
☐ 100 - 200 thousand. ☐ 100 - 200 million.
☐ 400 - 500 thousand. ☐ 500 - 1000 million.

49 Typhoid, paratyphoid and dysentery are known as f_____ b_____diseases.

50 For the multiplication of bacteria certain conditions are necessary.
_____ of the right kind.
_____ must be adequate.
_____ must be suitable.
_____ must elapse.

51 Are bacteria killed by cold? yes/no

52 Which of these foods are most easily contaminated?

Pork Pie   Trifle   Pickled Onions   Salt Beef

53 In which of the following should food not be stored and why?
☐ Larder ☐ Refrigerator ☐ Store ☐ Kitchen

54 Why should food be kept in a cool larder or refrigerator?

55 Which of the following provides an ideal heat for bacteria to grow?
☐ Cold soup ☐ Lukewarm soup ☐ Hot soup ☐ Boiling soup

56 State the temperatures between which bacteria multiply rapidly.
_____to _____.

57 Will bacteria remain dormant for long periods? yes/no

58 If foods have been contaminated before being made cold and kept in the refrigerator, on raising the temperature by keeping the foods in the kitchen for a period of time the bacteria will _____.

59 Bacteria require moisture for growth, they cannot multiply on dry food. true/false?

60 List four foods ideal for the growth of bacteria.
1   2   3   4

15

61 Indicate the foods which need the greatest care to prevent food poisoning.

☐ gravy ☐ milk ☐ dried peas ☐ jelly
☐ cream ☐ tea leaves ☐ aspic ☐ flour

62 Salmonella is the name of
☐ a patent fly catcher.
☐ the scientist who discovered food poisoning.
☐ living food poisoning bacteria.
☐ an insect spray fitted in kitchens.

63 Clostridium Welchii is now called
☐ perfecton.
☐ perfringens.
☐ ferpingons.
☐ ferfringens.

64 Explain the danger to humans of flies landing on food.

65 What is wrong and why?

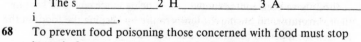

Raw chicken

Cooked meat

66 Germs present on human hands and other parts of the skin and in the nose or throat or sores and spots are S _____.

67 Food poisoning bacteria live in

1 The s_____ 2 H_____ 3 A_____;
i_____,

68 To prevent food poisoning those concerned with food must stop bacteria from_____and stop them from _____.

69 With what types of food poisoning are the following associated?

Flies

Insects

70 What is the responsibility of the carrier of an infectious disease?

71 Indicate how infection can be spread by
1 Humans
2 Animals, insects, birds
3 Inanimate objects (tea-towels, bowls, etc.)

72 The cook's best friend in the kitchen is a cat or small dog as they will help to kill the rats and mice. Discuss briefly.

73 State six ways to prevent infestation from vermin.

1	4
2	5
3	6

74 One of the most important ways to prevent contamination of food is by the correct _____ of food.

75 When cleaning pans used for porridge or starchy foods they are
☐ soaked in cold water.
☐ soaked in warm water.
☐ soaked in salt water.
☐ soaked in hot water.

76 The temperature of washing up water should be
☐ 62°C   ☐ 72°C   ☐ 82°C   ☐ 92°C

77 In which months of the year is extra care needed when storing foods?

78 What is wrong in this diagram?

79 Why may some shell fish such as oysters, mussels, cause food poisoning?

80 Which sauce made with eggs is liable to cause food poisoning? Describe briefly how this can happen.

81 Rechauffé indicates what kind of dish? _____

82 Milk to be safe should be
☐ pasteurised.   ☐ pacified.
☐ pasturised.   ☐ patronised.

83 Name four made-up dishes of food that require extra care in their preparation.
1   3
2   4

84 Tinned hams should be stored in the refrigerator. true/false?

85 Why should boned and rolled joints of meat require extra care in cooking?

86 Pork should always be well cooked. true/false?

87 Explain the reason for your answer to the previous question

88 Why do made-up fish dishes require special care and attention?

89 Why must watercress be thoroughly washed?

90 When handling left-over foods for re-use, if in doubts as to their freshness, what golden rule should you follow?

91 To whom should an employer report a case of typhoid?

92 List two items which should be available near to hand basins in kitchens?
1   2

18

93 Copies of the Food Hygiene Regulations may be obtained from HM
_____ Office.

94 What is the penalty for any person found guilty of an offence under
the Food Hygiene Regulations?

95 Name two institutions concerned with health and hygiene.
1
2

3 Gas and electricity

1 Write the method of transferring heat under the appropriate diagram.

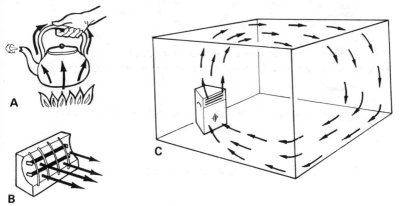

A

B

C

2 In the calculation of gas bills British Gas states the C_____
V_____ of the gas in B_____ T_____
U_____?

3 What is the purpose of a thermostat?
☐ To ignite the main jet.
☐ To control the pilot.
☐ To admit the air.
☐ To control the temperature.

4a The action of a rod-type thermostat depends upon the fact that some
metals expand more than others when heated. true/false?

b The action of a liquid thermostat depends upon the fact that a vapour
expands when heated. true/false?

19

5   Does air rise on being heated?

Electricity
1   Which of the following are insulators?
☐ rubber ☐ metal ☐ plastic ☐ glass ☐ tap water ☐ porcelain
2   The pressure of flow of electricity is measured by _____.
3   The rate of flow of electrical current is measured by _____.
4   The resistance of wires to the passage of electricity is measured by

_____.

5   To cut off the entire lighting or power circuit you would
☐ phone the Electricity Board.
☐ pull out all plugs and turn out all lights.
☐ pull down the main switch.
☐ sever the wires at the meter.
6   Read this meter.

Kilowatt
Hours
Reading = ... units

7   A fuse acts as a s_____ d_____.
8   Indicate which of the following cause blown fuses.
☐ Too many appliances plugged into a circuit
☐ By using a 5 ampere fuse on a lighting circuit
☐ Plugging a fire into a light socket
☐ Using a 10 amp fuse for an electric iron
☐ Short circuit due to insulation failure
☐ Switching off at the main suddenly
9   When repairing a fuse the first thing to do is
☐ stand on a non-conductor.
☐ turn off the main switch.
☐ phone for the electrician.
☐ turn off the appliance.
☐ put on rubber gloves.

10 When wiring a 13 amp plug, match

    1 Green/yellow   ☐ live

    2 Brown   ☐ neutral

    3 Blue   ☐ earth

11 An absorption type refrigerator has moving parts. true/false?

12 Deep-freezers should maintain temperatures of

    ☐ — 19°C.

    ☐ — 18°C.

    ☐ — 15°C.

    ☐ — 13°C.

4   Water

1 Wholesome water is free from

    1   3   5

    2   4

2 Water in certain districts is described as being hard.

Temporary hardness is caused by c_____ or m_____

b _____.

Permanent hardness is caused by s _____ or c_____ of

c_____ and m_____.

3 The Water Board's stopcock is situated

    ☐ in the cistern.   ☐ in the roof.

    ☐ inside the premises.   ☐ outside the premises.

4 When the ball arm of a ball valve lowers does it open or close the valve?

5 Flushing cisterns should discharge

    ☐ 1 gallon of water in 2 seconds.

    ☐ 2 gallons of water in 5 seconds.

    ☐ 5 gallons of water in 2 seconds.

    ☐ 2 gallons of water in 1 second.

6 Name the parts indicated by arrows.

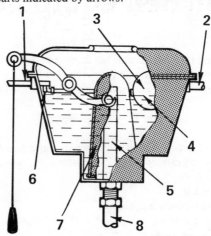

7 Washers for modern taps are obtainable in how many sizes?
☐ 1   ☐ 2   ☐ 3   ☐ 4

8 The stop-cock is also called the
☐ ball-valve   ☐ stop-valve
☐ stop-pipe

9 Why does the cold water flow into the bottom of the hot water storage tank?

10 An immersion heater may be connected to either the electricity or gas supply. true/false?

11 To clear a blocked sink, use a
☐ rubber water plunger   ☐ spider
☐ jelly bag   ☐ waste master

12 When water freezes it _____.

13 What is the reason for lagging water-pipes?

5   Kitchen equipment

pages 96-102

1   Why is the correct use, care and maintenance of kitchen equipment so important?

2   Add two points to the following which are important for the maintenance and care of kitchen equipment.
1   Periodic checks
2   Careful usage
3   Following maker's instructions
4   Reporting faults
5   Keeping a log book
6
7

3   Does a forced air convection oven have any advantage over a normally heated oven? yes/no

4   Briefly explain your answer to the previous question.

5   What advantage does a combination convection and microwave cooker have over an ordinary microwave cooker?

6   Microwave is a method of cooking and heating food by using
_____ power.

7   A microwave oven cooks food
☐ from the outside of the food.
☐ the whole food at the same time.
☐ just the inside.
☐ only the outside.

8   What is the chief advantage of cooking by microwave?

9   State two advantages of the induction cooker.
1
2

10 Which is the odd one and why in relation to microwave cookery?
glassware, silverware, plastic container, paper container,
earthenware, chinaware.

11 The bratt pan may be used for five different methods of cookery.

1   3   5

2   4

12 What other advantage has the bratt pan?

13 Why is the steam jacket boiler most suitable for cooking large
quantities of food with a thickened content?

14 What is the purpose of the 'cool zone' in a deep fat fryer?

15 Put the names below the appropriate illustrations.
boiling pan   bratt pan   deep fat fryer
salamander   steamer   microwave oven
high pressure steamer

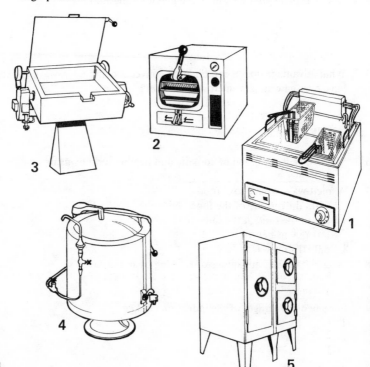

15 What is the purpose of the hot plate (hot cupboard)?

16 A bain-marie is used for
☐ washing vegetables ☐ basting meat
☐ keeping food hot ☐ pot washing

17 A double sided or infra-grill is suitable for a fast food operation.
true/false?

18 Match the following.
Salamander ☐ 1 Heat above and below
Grill ☐ 2 Heat above
Contact grill ☐ 3 Heat under

19 Match the following.
☐ Stainless steel sink 1 General light purpose
☐ Glazed earthenware sink 2 Heavy pot wash
☐ Galvanised iron sink 3 General purpose

20 On which of the following surfaces would you cut with a knife?
☐ Wooden table ☐ Cutting board
☐ Stainless steel ☐ Marble

21 Hot pans should be placed on a _____ on the table in order
to protect the table surface.

22 List three points to observe when cleaning a butcher's block.
1
2
3

23 Name three factors that should influence the decision whether to use
an item of mechanical equipment.
1 Can it save _____
2 Can it save _____
3 Can it produce a _____ _____ _____

24 Before loading potatoes into the potato peeler _____ and
_____.

25 In order to maintain a refrigerator at peak efficiency it should be
defrosted
☐ daily. ☐ weekly. ☐ monthly. ☐ every two months.

26 Defrosting of a refrigerator is necessary in order to
produce more ice cubes.
stop foods from freezing hard.
provide a supply of distilled water.
prevent overworking of the motor.

27 Food should be tightly packed into the refrigerator in order to
maximise its use. true/false?

28 Name six examples of use of a food mixing machine.
1 4
2 5
3 6

29 What can be the effect of overloading the mincer attachment of a food mixing machine?

30 What is the greatest potential danger to a food handler when operating a food slicing or chopping machine?

31 List five power-driven machines described as dangerous.
1   2
2   4
5

32 Working instructions should be placed in a _____ position near the machines.

33 How is milk heated in a still set?

34 The draw-off taps on coffee and milk storage chambers in still sets should be cleaned by
☐ pushing a piece of bent wire through.   ☐ using a special brush.
☐ pushing a piece of clean muslin through.   ☐ pouring through a strong detergent solution.

35 What are the generally recognised requirements for hygienic washing up?
A good supply of_____water at a temperature of 60°C for general c_____followed by a _____rinse at a temperature of 82°C for at least _____ _____.

36 Name the three main types of dishwashing machines.
1   2   3

37 Food waste disposers are the most modern and hygienic method of waste disposal. true/false?

38 Almost every type of rubbish and swill can be finely ground down and rinsed down the drain by food waste disposers, but what are the two exceptions to this?
1   2

39 How would you prove an omelet pan?

40 Name four different types of frying pan.
1   2   3   4

41 A conical strainer is used for _____ _____
_____.

42 When is the only time that a sieve should be used upside down?

43   Re-arrange the captions in correct order.

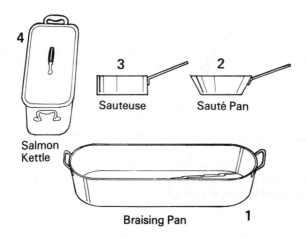

44   What are the advantages of copper equipment?

45   What are the disadvantages of copper equipment?

46   Copper pans are lined with tin. true/false?
47   Give the French names for six copper pans.

1	4
2	5
3	6

48   Name two items of copper equipment that are not lined with tin.
1   2
49   1/3 _____   1/3 _____   1/3 _____
make a paste with vinegar suitable for cleaning copper pans.
50   Why should the use of metal spoons or whisks be avoided with
aluminium pans?

51   Is water boiled in aluminium pans suitable for making tea?
yes/no
52   Is stainless steel a good conductor of heat?
53   Why do some stainless steel pans have a thick layer of copper in the
base?
54   Non-stick pans are best cleaned with
☐ wire wool   ☐ kitchen paper
☐ Brillo pad   ☐ cleaning powder

55 State the most suitable material with the utensil.

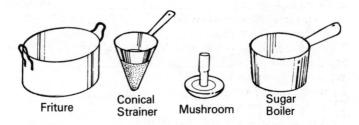

Friture   Conical Strainer   Mushroom   Sugar Boiler

56 What four points should be observed in order to prevent warping and splintering of cutting boards?
1
2
3
4

57 Name three materials from which piping bags are made.
1   2   3

6 Elementary nutrition and food science

1 Give a brief definition of food.

2 List the six nutrients.
1   4
2   5
3   6

3 The study of nutrients is known as _____.

4 Which food contains only one nutrient?
☐ egg   ☐ sugar
☐ apple   ☐ flour

5 For the body to obtain maximum benefit from food it is essential that everyone concerned with the buying, storage, cooking and serving of food and the compiling of menus should have some knowledge of

_____.

6   Digestion is the _____ of the _____.
7   Digestion takes place in the mouth where s _____ is added,
    in the stomach where g _____ j _____ are added
    and in the small intestine where the n _____ are broken
    down further and additional j _____ are added.
8   To enable the body to benefit from food it must be absorbed into the
    blood stream. true/false?
9   When does absorption take place?
    ☐ When drinking with food.
    ☐ At the same time as digestion.
    ☐ After the food has been broken down.
    ☐ Just before digestion.
10 If the body is to obtain full benefit from foods, then the foods must
    s _____, l _____ and taste attractive.
11 What do you understand by a state of malnutrition?

12 Re-arrange the following tables of the main functions of nutrients
    correctly.

Energy	*Growth and repair*	*Regulation of body processes*
Proteins	Water	Minerals
Fats	Carbohydrates	Proteins
Vitamins	Minerals	Water

13 Name the two kinds of protein.
    1   2
14 Protein is needed for _____ of the body and for the
    _____ of body tissues.
15 Do growing children and expectant mothers need more protein than
    other adults. yes/no
16 Explain the reason for your answer to the previous question.

17 List four foods that give the main supply of protein in the average diet.
    1   3
    2   4
18 Protein is composed of _____ acids.
19 All these acids are essential to the body. true/false?

20 The protein of cheese is different from the protein of meat because the arrangement of the _____ is not the same.

21 Which is the odd one out and why?

22 Moderately cooked protein is most easy to digest. true/false?

23 Give an example to illustrate your answer to the previous question.

24 What are the two main groups of fats? _____

25 The function of fats is to
1 protect vital _____ of the body;
2 provide heat and _____;
3 in the case of certain fats provide _____.

26 Indicate the origin of the following foods by writing A for animal and V for vegetable.

   ☐ butter   ☐ soya bean   ☐ olive oil   ☐ herring
   ☐ cod liver oil   ☐ suet   ☐ meat fat   ☐ cream
   ☐ margarine   ☐ nuts   ☐ lard   ☐ dripping
   ☐ sun flower oil ☐ bacon   ☐ halibut liver oil ☐ cheese

27 Olive oil is a fat which is liquid at room temperature. true/false?

28 Which is the odd one out and why?

Herring   BUTTER   Walnuts   Olives   Black Currants   Avocado Pear

29 Fats differ because of the _____ acids from which they are derived.

30 Give three examples of fatty acids.

1   3

2

31 Fatty acids affect the _____ and _____ of the fat.

32 Fats provide the body with _____ and _____.

33 List six oily fish.

1   4

2   5

3   6

34 Name the three main groups of carbohydrates.

1   2   3

35 The function of carbohydrates is to provide the body with most of its

☐ vitamins   ☐ carbon

☐ protection   ☐ energy

36 Name three foods which are main suppliers of carbohydrate in the diet.

1   2   3

37 Sugar is the simplest form of carbohydrate. true/false?

38 Match the following.

1 Maltose   ☐ Beet and cane sugar

2 Lactose   ☐ Fruit

3 Sucrose   ☐ Milk

4 Glucose   ☐ Honey and animal blood

5 Fructose   ☐ Grain

39 Which of the following foods contribute starch to the diet?

☐ Rice   ☐ Peas

☐ Beef   ☐ Butter beans

☐ Flour   ☐ Onions

☐ Plaice   ☐ Apples

40 Give three examples of foods containing starch in each of the following categories.

	1	2	3
Whole grains	1	2	3
Powdered grains	1	2	3
Vegetables	1	2	3
Unripe fruit	1	2	3
Cereals	1	2	3
Cooked starch	1	2	3
Pasta	1	2	3

41 Cellulose is the

☐ skin of fresh fish   ☐ coarser structure of vegetables and cereals

☐ sinew of meat   ☐ most complex of all the vitamins.

42 What is the purpose of cellulose in the diet?

43 Which is the odd one out and why?

44 Vitamins are the chemical substances which are _____ for life.

45 Vitamins are produced both naturally and synthetically. true/false?

46 Give two examples of the general function of vitamins.
1   2

47 In which of the following is Vitamin A found?
☐ Liver   ☐ Cooking fat   ☐ Carrots   ☐ Cauliflower
☐ Lamb   ☐ Herrings   ☐ Apricots   ☐ Milk
☐ Butter   ☐ Plaice   ☐ Cheese   ☐ Cherries

48 Vitamin A is fat soluble. true/false?

49 List three functions of vitamins.
1   2   3

50 Which vitamin is necessary for healthy bones and teeth?

51 Which two vitamins are added to margarine?
1   2

52 Name the most important source of vitamin D.

53 Name three groups of foods containing vitamin D.
1   2   3

54 Is vitamin B required to enable the body to obtain energy from the carbohydrates. yes/no?

55 Name three foods in which vitamin B is found.
1   2   3

56 List the three main substances which make up the vitamin B group.
1   2   3

57 Can vitamin B be lost in cooking. yes/no?

58 Indicate by using initials which of the following foods are sources of B1 Thiamine (T), Riboflavine (R) or Niacin (N).
☐ wholemeal bread ☐ bacon ☐ yeast ☐ oatmeal
☐ cheese ☐ liver ☐ meat extract ☐ beef
☐ egg ☐ kidney ☐ peas ☐ brewers' yeast

59 What is another name for Niacin?

60 Vitamin C can be lost in cooking and by bad s _____.

61 Name six foods containing vitamin C.
1   3   5
2   4   6

62 Match the following
☐ Egg yolk   1 Vitamin A
☐ Kidney   2 Vitamin B
☐ Oranges   3 Vitamin C
☐ Yeast   4 Vitamin D

63 Which three of the following mineral elements are most likely to be deficient in the diet?
☐ Calcium   ☐ Phosphorous   ☐ Iron
☐ Sodium   ☐ Potassium   ☐ Iodine

64 List three sources of each of the mineral elements selected in the previous question.

65 The use that the body makes of calcium is dependent upon the present of vitamin _____.

66 Name two foods that are sources of calcium.
1   2

67 What is the mineral element needed particularly for growing bones and teeth and for expectant and nursing mothers?

68 The body makes use of phosphorus in conjunction with c _____ _____ and vitamin _____.

69 Which four of the following foods are sources of phosphorus?
☐ Liver   ☐ Eggs   ☐ Fish
☐ Cheese   ☐ Lettuce   ☐ Spinach

70 Iron is required for building the haemoglobin in blood and is therefore necessary for transporting _____ and _____ _____ round the body.

71 Which three of the following foods are sources of iron?
☐ Lean meat ☐ Offal ☐ Egg yolk
☐ Tomatoes ☐ Carrots ☐ Cream

72 Which mineral element is found in all body fluids and is found as salt?

73 Which mineral element do we lose from the body when we perspire?

74 Water is required for which body functions?
M _____ B _____ F _____
A _____ E _____
D _____ S _____

75 Excluding liquids, name six foods that contain water.
1   3   5
2   4   6

76 Match the following.
1 Protein   ☐ nutritive value not affected by normal cooking.
2 Carbohydrate   ☐ lost by cooking and keeping hot.
3 Fat   ☐ destroyed by high temperature and use of
                   bicarbonate of soda.
4 Iron   ☐ may be acquired from pans in which cooked.
5 Vitamin B1   ☐ needs to be thoroughly cooked.
6 Vitamin C   ☐ overcooking reduces nutritive value.

77 What effect does overcooking have on the nutritive value of food?

78 Unless starch is thoroughly cooked it cannot be properly digested.
true/false?

79 Is the nutritive value of fat affected by cooking? yes/no

80 Which of the following vitamins can withstand cooking temperatures
and are not lost in cooking?
Vitamins   ☐ A   ☐ B   ☐ C   ☐ D

81 Why is energy required by the body?

82 Foods containing a high fat content will have a high _____
content.
Foods containing a lot of water will have a low _____
content.

83 By which term is the energy value of food measured?
☐ Calcium ☐ Celanus
☐ Calcius ☐ Calorie

84 People engaged in energetic work require more calories than people
engaged in sedentary occupations. true/false?

85 Who needs the highest daily calorie intake?
A young male apprentice aged 19 playing football two evenings a week.
A young lady receptionist who attends a disco once a week.
An office typist who is a keen television fan.
An accountant who is studying hard for examinations.

86 _____ is said to be the almost perfect food.

87 Why is margarine sometimes more nutritious than butter?

88 Why is the food value of cheese exceptional?

89 What does bacon contain nutritionally that is not present in other meats?

90 Cheaper cuts of meat are less nourishing than dearer cuts of meat. true/false?

91 Sweetbreads are valuable to invalids because they
□ look appetising.   □ are easily digested.
□ are very tasty.   □ are highly nutritious.

92 When bones of tinned salmon or sardines are eaten, they are a source of calcium. true/false?

93 Which of the following is correct?
□ Fish is a more valuable source of protein than meat.
□ Fish is equally valuable as a source of protein as meat.
□ Fish is a less valuable source of protein than meat.
□ Fish is not a source of protein at all.

94 The oil in oily fish is contained in the liver. true/false?

95 The carbohydrate in unripe fruit is in the form of _____
which changes to _____ when the fruit is ripe.

96 Which is the odd one out and why?
Oranges   Lemons   Strawberries
Blackcurrants   Pears   Grapefruit

97 Nuts are a source of cellulose. true/false?

98 Green vegetables are valuable because they contain which of the following vitamins and minerals?
□ Iron, calcium, vitamins A and C.
□ Phosphorus, calcium, vitamins A and D.
□ Iron, calcium, vitamins B and C.
□ Iodine, sodium, vitamins A and D.

99 Potatoes are a valuable source of vitamin D because they are eaten in large quantities. true/false?

100 State the main value of onions in cookery.

101 Which vitamin is contained in wholemeal flour?

102 Saccharine has no food value. true/false?

103 What food value have tea and coffee?

104 When compiling a balanced diet, in which order are the following considered?
☐ Body building foods.
☐ Energy producing foods.
☐ Protective foods.

7 Commodities

1 Meat

1 Why is it necessary to know and understand the structure of meat in order to cook it properly?

2 Lean flesh is composed of m_____which are numerous bundles of f _____ held together by connective tissue.

3 The size of the fibres in meat affects the grain and texture of the meat. true/false?

4 There are two kinds of connective tissue, the yellow e _____ and the white c _____.

5 The quantity of connective tissue that binds the fibres together has much to do with the tenderness and eating quality of the meat. true/false?

6 As the yellow connective tissue will not cook, how must it be dealt with?

7 When the white connective tissue is cooked it decomposes in moist heat to form g _____.

8 The quantity and quality of fat are important factors in determining eating quality of meat. true/false?

9 Briefly discuss the previous question.

10 Meat is hung to
   ☐ increase the leanness.
   ☐ enable the blood to congeal.
   ☐ increase the flavour and tenderness.
   ☐ facilitate jointing.

11 Briefly discuss your answer to the previous question.

12 Meat is generally hung at a temperature of
   ☐ −1°C   ☐ 1°C   ☐ 2°C   ☐ 4°C

13 Match the following
   ☐ Pig   1 Lamb and mutton
   ☐ Calf   2 Pork and bacon
   ☐ Sheep   3 Veal

14 *La viande* is French for _____.

15 List four points to consider when storing fresh meat.
   1   3
   2   4

16 List four points to consider when storing fresh bacon.
   1   3
   2   4

17 Describe how you would recognise good quality beef.

18 Are supplies of home produced veal obtainable all year round? yes/no

19 The quality of veal necessary for first class cookery requires a carcass of meat weighing approximately 100 kg. true/false?

20 Would veal described as pale pink, firm and moist with firm pinkish white fat be of good or poor quality?

21 Could Britain be called a lamb eating country?

22 Although in Britain we produce much of our own lamb and mutton, from which other country do we import large quantities?

23 Lamb is the term given to animals not more than:-
☐ 1 year old   ☐ 1½ years old
☐ 2 years old   ☐ 3 years old

24 Good quality lamb should have
☐ lean, firm, bright red fine grain flesh, hard white evenly distributed fat.
☐ lean, soft, bright red fine grain flesh, hard white evenly distributed fat.
☐ lean, soft, dull red fine grain flesh, hard white evenly distributed fat.
☐ lean, firm, dull red fine grain flesh, hard white evenly distributed fat.

25 Pork must always be well cooked because
☐ otherwise it will be greasy and tasteless.
☐ that is the way customers like it.
☐ otherwise it will be tough and stringy.
☐ because *trichinae* (parasitic worms) may be present and must be destroyed by heat.

26 Briefly describe good quality pork.

27 Briefly describe the two methods of curing bacon.

28 Green bacon has a milder flavour than smoked bacon. true/false?
29 Bacon is the cured flesh of the baconer pig. true/false?
30 Ham is the hind leg of
☐ porker pig, cut square, pickled, dried and smoked.
☐ baconer pig, cut square, pickled, dried and smoked.
☐ porker pig, cut round with the aitchbone, pickled, dried and smoked.
☐ baconer pig, cut round with the aitchbone, pickled, dried and smoked.

31 All hams must be well cooked before being eaten. true/false?

32 What is the food value of meat?

33 List four ways of preserving meat.
1   3
2   4

34 What is meant by chilled meat?

35 Which one of the diagrams below is correct according to the key?

1 ☐   2 ☐   3 ☐   4 ☐   A   Leg   E   Shoulder
                                 B   Breast   F   Scrag End
                                 C   Middle Neck G   Best End
                                 D   Saddle

2   Offal

36 The edible parts taken from the inside of the carcass are called

37 State the names of four items referred to in the previous question.
1   2   3   4

38 Tripe is the _____ lining or white _____ of the ox.

39 The best tripe is
☐ Honeydew   ☐ Velvet
☐ Honeycomb   ☐ Smooth

40 Oxtails should be of good size, meaty and lean. true/false?

41 Give one use for each of the following.
1   sheep's head   _____
2   calf's head   _____
3   pig's head   _____

42   Give three quality points and one use for beef suet

      1

      2

      3

      Use

43   From where is beef marrow obtained?

44   Name one use for each of the following.

      1 lamb's kidney

      2 calf's kidney

      3 sheep's kidney

      4 ox kidney

      5 pig's kidney

45   The food value of kidney is similar to liver. true/false?

46   The hearts of which two animals are sometimes used in cookery?

      1   2

47   The tongue of which animal is popular both as a hot and cold meat?

48   Ox-tongues must be salted before being used. true/false?

49   Sweetbreads are

      ☐ glands which when cooked are nutritious and digestible.

      ☐ small balls of stuffing served with chicken.

      ☐ offal obtained from suckling pigs.

      ☐ glands from the pancreas and heart used for diets.

      ☐ sweet tasting stomach lining.

50   Heart sweetbreads are superior in quality to the neck sweetbreads. true/false?

3 **Poultry**

1   Poultry is the term which covers

      ☐ domestic birds which are free ranging.

      ☐ edible domestic birds and wild birds.

      ☐ edible birds which have finished laying.

      ☐ domestic birds bred to be eaten.

2   Indicate the correct poultry quality points.

      ☐ The bird's breast should be plump.

      ☐ The flesh should be firm.

      ☐ The vent-end of the breastbone must be pliable.

      ☐ The skin should be white and unbroken.

      ☐ Young birds have spurs and large scales on their legs.

3   The flesh of poultry is more easily digested than that of butcher's
       meat. true/false?

4   Unlike meat, fresh poultry need not be hung. true/false?

5   Frozen birds must be kept in the deep freeze unit until required to be
       defrosted. true/false?

6   When de-frosting birds it is best to
       ☐ place them in warm water.
       ☐ place them in cold water.
       ☐ place them on the kitchen table.
       ☐ place them in the refrigerator.

7   Match the following.
       1   Baby (spring) chicken   ☐ Broiler
       2   Capon   ☐ Old hen
       3   Boiling fowl   ☐ 4 - 6 weeks old
       4   Medium roasting chicken   ☐ Large roasting bird

8   The smallest chicken is known as a _____.

9   The largest chicken is known as a _____.

10 Put in order of size - smallest first.
       Turkey ☐   Duck ☐   Quail ☐   Poussin ☐

11 Turkeys are available in weights from_____to_____.

12 Give three quality points for prime turkey.
       1
       2
       3

13 What is grey and white, feathered and resembles a chicken?

4   **Game**

1   State five points to look for in quality of game birds.
       1   4
       2   5
       3

2   What do you understand by the term game?

3   Name the two groups into which game can be divided.
       1   2

4   Is game less or more fat than poultry or meat?

5   Game is easily digested. true/false?

6   Game birds and game animals are hung with their fur/feathers on.
       true/false?

7   Game must be hung to enable it to become_____and to
       develop _____.

8   What are the four factors that determine the hanging time for game?

     1   t _____

     2   c _____

     3   a _____

     4   s _____ t _____

9   Place the following in order of size - smallest first.

Wild duck ☐	Pheasant ☐	Partridge ☐
Grouse ☐	Woodcock ☐	Wood pigeon ☐

10   What is the name given to the flesh of deer?

11   Give two quality points for joints of venison

     1   Well f _____

     2   Dark b_____ r_____colour

12   Venison is

    ☐ old veal.

    ☐ a type of pâté.

    ☐ a type of Scottish beef,

    ☐ the flesh of deer.

13   Why is venison marinaded before being cooked?

    ☐ To kill parasites

    ☐ To help its keeping quality

    ☐ To counteract toughness and dryness

    ☐ To form the base of the gravy

14   Of what significance are the ears of hares and rabbits?

15   What two kinds of rabbits are used for cooking?

16   With what are woodcock and snipe trussed?

5   **Fish**

1   Which is the odd one out and why?

    Haddock   Herring   Cod   Whiting   Hake

2   What have the following in common?

    Plaice   Brill   Sole   Turbot   Dab

3 The approximate loss from boning and waste in the preparation of flat fish fillets is

☐ 10%   ☐ 20%   ☐ 30%   ☐ 50%

4 The approximate loss from boning and waste in the preparation of round fish fillets is

☐ 60%   ☐ 40%   ☐ 20%   ☐ 10%

5 Halibut and cod liver contain _____

6 State six points to be observed when purchasing fish.

1   4

2   5

3   6

7 Which vitamins are contained in fish?

8 What is a buckling?

9 Name three fish which are canned.

1   2   3

10 Kippers are produced from

☐ codling.   ☐ herring.

☐ whiting.   ☐ haddock.

11 Name three fish which may be smoked.

1   2   3

12 Caviar is obtained from

☐ salmon.   ☐ skate.

☐ sturgeon.   ☐ hake.

13 The conger eel is larger than the eel. true/false?

14 Mackerel must be used fresh because the flesh _____ very quickly.

15 Name three British rivers in which salmon are fished.

1   2   3

16 Rollmops are

☐ pickled rolled sprat fillets.

☐ pickled rolled herring fillets.

☐ pickled rolled haddock fillets.

☐ smoked herring fillets.

17 Name three fish which may be eaten smoked and which are not cooked apart from this smoking process.

1   2   3

18 What have the following in common?

Anchovies   Eels   Herring   Salmon   Sprats   Tunny fish

19 Which fish is served jellied? _____

43

20 A salmon weighing less than 3½ kg is known as a _____.

21 The sea-fish similar in appearance to salmon is
☐ tunny.   ☐ rainbow trout.
☐ trout.   ☐ salmon trout.

22 Sardines are only used when tinned. true/false

23 Are trout fished from rivers, lakes or the sea?

24 Which fish is used for serving *au bleu*?

25 What is tunny?
☐ Baby turbot   ☐ A very large fish
☐ A quantity of trout   ☐ A kind of fishing boat

26 Which is the turbot and which is the brill?

27 Whitebait are the fry of young _____.

28 Whitebait can be cooked in a variety of ways. true/false?

29 Name the fish which was 'wings'.

30 Halibut is a white flat fish which can weigh up to
☐ 50 kg   ☐ 75 kg   ☐ 100 kg   ☐ 150 kg

31 Which is considered to be the best of the flat fish?
☐ Plaice   ☐ Dover sole   ☐ Lemon sole   ☐ Witch

32 What is the current market price of Dover sole?

33 The average weight of a turbot is
☐ ½ - 1 kg   ☐ 1½ - 2 kg
☐ 2½ - 3 kg   ☐ 3½ - 4 kg

34 Name three popular round sea-fish.
1   2   3

35 Explain what is meant by *en goujons*?

36 How can you distinguish a whole cod from a whole haddock?

37 Which of the following is easy to digest and therefore suitable for invalid cookery?
☐ Red mullet　　　　　☐ Herring
☐ Salmon　　　　　　☐ Whiting

38 What is the purchasing unit of oysters?
☐ Singles　　　　　　☐ ½ dozen
☐ Tens　　　　　　　☐ Dozens

39 Shellfish is easily digested. true/false?

40 Why is a little vinegar used in the cooking of shellfish?

41 Why if possible, is it best to buy shellfish alive?

42 Arrange the following in order of size - smallest first.
☐ Shrimps　　☐ Lobster　　☐ Prawn　　☐ Crawfish

43 The colour of live lobster is
☐ red.　　　☐ orange.　　☐ green.　　☐ bluish black.

44 Hen lobsters are distinguished from cock lobsters by broader/ narrower tail?

45 From which lobster can we obtain coral? hen/cock

46 Identify the following.

A　　　　　　B　　　C　　　　D　　E

47   The name given to shell fish soup is
☐ Soupe   ☐ Purée   ☐ Velouté   ☐

48   Which is a crawfish and which a crayfish?

A

B

49   There is usually more flesh on a hen crab but the flesh is considered to be of inferior quality to that of the cock crab. true/false?

50   By what two features of the crab tail can you distinguish a hen crab from a cock crab?
1
2

51   Which is the odd one out and why?
Whitstable,   Chelmsford,   Colchester,   Helford.

52   The majority of oysters eaten in Britain are consumed raw. true/false?

53   When are English oysters in season? _____

54   Name two countries from which we import oysters during the summer months.
1   2

55   Name two essential purchasing points of quality for mussels.
1   2

56   Mussels may be served hot or cold. true/false?

57   Why are scallops so dirty when fished out of the sea?

58   Why do we retain the deep shell of the scallop?

59 Name two fish roes that are popular eaten on their own.
1   2

6   **Vegetables**
1   What is the nutritional value of root vegetables?

2   List ten vegetables available all the year round.
1   3   5   7   9
2   4   6   8   10
3   Little protein or carbohydrate is found in green vegetables. true/false?
4   Fresh green vegetables are rich in _____ and _____.
5   Describe good quality cabbage in four or five words.

6   Fresh green vegetables should be stored in
☐ the containers they are delivered in.
☐ on well ventilated racks.
☐ vegetable bins.
☐ the refrigerator.
7   Fresh vegetables and fruit are living _____ and will lose
_____ quickly if not properly _____ and handled.
8   Because of air cargo transport many fruits and vegetables are in season
the whole year round. true/false?
9   Name two types of artichoke.
1   2
10 Name three types of fresh beans.
1   2   3
11 What are the two chief types of mushrooms?
1   2
12 What are two alternative names for sweetcorn?

13 Name three types of vegetables that can be purchased in dehydrated
form?
1   2   3
14 Tick the methods by which vegetables are preserved.
☐ canning   ☐ pickling   ☐ freezing   ☐ dehydrating
☐ drying   ☐ smoking   ☐ salting
15 Name three vegetables available in dried form.
1   2   3
16 Name three popular pickled vegetables.
1   2   3
17 Name six vegetables available in deep-frozen form.
1   3   5
2   4   6

18 What is the difference between a cos and a cabbage lettuce?

19 Which group is obtainable fresh in winter?
- [ ] sprouts, celery, swedes, parsnips
- [ ] marrow, sprouts, asparagus, cabbage
- [ ] runner beans, carrots, swedes, sweetcorn
- [ ] peas, parsnips, aubergine, seakale

7 **Fruit**

20 Give two examples of each fruit classification.

	1	2
Soft fruit	1	2
Hard fruit	1	2
Stone fruit	1	2
Citrus fruit	1	2
Tropical	1	2

21 Name four English soft fruits in addition to the two in the previous question.

1   3
2   4

22 Which are the three most used citrus fruits?

1   2   3

23 Are the fruits given in your previous answer available all the year round. yes/no?

24 Rhubarb is in season during
- [ ] Autumn
- [ ] Spring
- [ ] Winter
- [ ] Summer

25 From which month do English soft fruits come into season?
- [ ] April
- [ ] July
- [ ] June
- [ ] August

26 Place the following in order of availability during the year.
- [ ] gooseberries
- [ ] cherries
- [ ] damsons
- [ ] currants
- [ ] raspberries
- [ ] plums

27 Imported apples and pears are available all the year round. true/false?

28 Which of the following fruit are available in dried form?
- [ ] apples
- [ ] gooseberries
- [ ] apricots
- [ ] damsons
- [ ] strawberries
- [ ] pears
- [ ] rhubarb
- [ ] figs

29 Plums when dried are called

30 Small grapes when dried are called

31 Medium-sized grapes when dried are called

32 Large grapes when dried are called

33 Solid packed apples are apples which have been peeled, cored, quartered and
- ☐ packed tightly in cases.
- ☐ frozen and packed in water in tins.
- ☐ packed in water in tins.
- ☐ packed in large barrels.

34 What are candied, glacé and crystallised fruits?

35 Citrus fruits are a source of vitamin _____.

36 Bananas should be stored in a refrigerator. true/false?

37 Give an example of a different fruit bought in each of the following.

a tray   a case

a punnet   a box

38 Give an example of a

candied fruit

crystallised fruit

glacé fruit

39 From which country do we import most of our glacé, crystallised and candied fruit?

☐ Italy	☐ Holland
☐ Spain	☐ France

40 What kinds of fruits are the following?

Blenheim Orange   William

Bramley's seedling   Avocado

Comice   Cantaloup

41 Give the name of a chicken dish which includes banana as part of the garnish.

42 Name a fish dish garnished with banana.

43 Name three fruits which have both dessert and cooking varieties.

1   2   3

44 Marmalade can be made from

1   2   3

45 Bananas can be grilled, fried or eaten raw. true/false?

46 Which fruit is used to garnish fish Véronique?

47 Name three types of melon

1   2   3

48 Is a honeydew melon round or oval?

49 Which fruit berry sauce is served with roast turkey?
☐ blackberry
☐ cranberry
☐ gooseberry
☐ mulberry

50 Name two varieties of each fruit below.

A   B   C

8 **Nuts**

50 Nuts are a source of

51 When purchasing nuts select those which are heavy for their size.
true/false?

52 Name three popular dessert nuts.
1   2   3

53 Which nut has probably the most uses in pastry and confectionery
work?
☐ Almond   ☐ Brazil
☐ Walnut   ☐ Pecan

54 Give four examples of the use of nuts in pastry work.
1
2
3
4

55 Which nut is used in desiccated form for certain curry dishes?

56 Small green nuts used for decorating are called
☐ Filberts   ☐ Adagio
☐ Cobs   ☐ Pistachio

57 Name three types of nuts that are served salted.
1   2   3

50

58 Match the correct names to these nuts.

Chestnut	Walnut	Coconut	Almond	Brazil
1	2	3	4	5

9 **Eggs**

1 When assessing quality points for buying eggs, the eggshell should be c_____n, well s_____d, s_____g and slightly r_____h.

2 When an egg is broken, if it is fresh, there ought to be a high p_____n of thick w_____e to thin w_____e.

3 The yolk should be f_____m, r_____d and of good e_____n c_____r.

4 What happens to the white of egg if it is kept too long?

5 What happens to the yolk of egg if the egg is kept too long?

6 Eggs should be stored in a
☐ cold, very dry place.   ☐ cool, dry place.
☐ cold, damp place.   ☐ cool but not too dry place.

7 The ideal storage place for eggs is in a refrigerator without any strong smelling foods at a temperature of
☐ 0° - 5°   ☐ 18° - 20°
☐ 10° - 15°   ☐ 22° - 25°

8 Why should strong smelling foods not be stored near eggs?

9 Give three examples of strong smelling foods which should not be stored near eggs.
1   2   3

10 If there were a shortage of hen's eggs, which other two birds' eggs could be used in place?
1 t_____ 2 g_____ f_____

11 State the nutritional value of eggs.

12 Give examples of the uses of eggs.

    e.g.   thickening   -   baked egg custard, mayonnaise

          clarifying   -

          binding   -

          coating   -

          colouring   -

10   **Milk**

13 Why is milk regarded as the almost perfect food?

14 Unlike eggs, milk will not absorb strong smells from other foods if kept uncovered in a refrigerator. true/false?

17 Milk is pasteurised in order to

  ☐ improve its keeping quality.

  ☐ improve its flavour.

  ☐ concentrate the strength.

  ☐ to kill harmful bacteria.

18 Pasteurised milk is heated for

  ☐ 15 seconds at 72°C

  ☐ 20 seconds at 52°C

  ☐ 25 seconds at 62°C

  ☐ 30 seconds at 72°C

19 What is U.H.T. milk?

20 Under sterile conditions U.H.T. milk will keep for

  ☐ 2 - 3 days.

  ☐ 6 - 7 days.

  ☐ 9 - 10 days.

  ☐ 2 - 3 weeks.

21 Homogenised milk has been

  ☐ pasteurised twice.

  ☐ drawn from a herd of pedigree cows.

  ☐ treated so that the cream is dispersed throughout the milk.

  ☐ pasteurised and U.H.T. treated.

22 Sterilised milk is produced from milk which has been

  ☐ homogenised.

  ☐ pasteurised.

  ☐ condensed.

  ☐ evaporated.

23 What is the ingredient in cream that causes it to be able to be whipped?   B_____

24   What is the essential difference between single and double cream?

25   Devonshire and clotted cream are two different names for the same type of cream. true/false?

26   With what would clotted cream be served?

27   If cream is overwhipped it turns to
    ☐ yoghurt.
    ☐ margarine.
    ☐ cheese.
    ☐ butter.

28   Is there any remedy for over-whipped fresh cream. yes/no?

29   When whipping fresh cream the cream must be
    ☐ warm.   ☐ cold.
    ☐ at blood heat.   ☐ almost frozen.

30   Yoghurt is prepared from milk. true/false?

11   **Fats and oils**

31   Fats should be kept in a cold store or refrigerator. true/false?

32   Why should butter be kept away from strong smelling foods?

33   It takes approximately _____ litre of cream to produce _____ kg of butter.

34   Butter is an e _____ y food because it has a very high f _____ content.

35   If kept too long butter becomes
    ☐ saturated.   ☐ liquid.
    ☐ rancid.   ☐ pasteurised.

36   Why is salt added to some makes of butter in its production?

37   Butter is imported in large amounts from all but one of the following countries. Indicate the odd one out.
    ☐ New Zealand   ☐ France   ☐ Denmark
    ☐ Australia   ☐ Austria   ☐ Holland

38   Butter when used for shallow frying is
    ☐ homogenised.   ☐ condensed.
    ☐ sterilised.   ☐ clarified.

39   Margarine is nutritionally inferior to butter. true/false?

40   Margarine is manufactured from whole cream, milk and a v _____ oil.

41   Margarine can be used in place of butter for all culinary purposes. true/false?

42 Name three types of oil used to produce margarine.

1   2   3

43 Lard is the rendered fat from

☐ ox   ☐ pig

☐ sheep   ☐ goat

44 The fat content of lard is almost

☐ 100%   ☐ 90%   ☐ 80%   ☐ 70%

45 Suet is obtained from the

☐ kidney region of baconer pigs.

☐ liver region of pork.

☐ heart region of veal.

☐ kidney region of beef.

46 Clarified animal fat is called?

47 Oils are fats which are liquid at room temperature. true/false?

48 Name three varieties of vegetable oil.

1   2   3

49 Will a good vegetable oil keep indefinitely at room temperature. yes/no?

50 Which of the vegetable oils is considered to have the best flavour?

☐ olive   ☐ groundnut   ☐ maize

51 Name three countries from which olive oil is imported.

1   2   3

52 The best oils are almost free from

1   2   3

53 What is an essential requirement for an oil that is to be used for deep-frying?

54 Which of the following would you use for deep-frying?

☐ vegetable oil   ☐ dripping

☐ maize oil   ☐ olive oil

55 Give the reason for your answer to the previous question.

56 Why should oils be free from moisture?

12 Cheese

57 Cheese is made from _____.

58 List the four main types of cheese and give an example of each.

1

2

3

4

59 Which cheese is made from goat's milk?
☐ Parmesan ☐ Edam
☐ Parisienne ☐ Brie

60 Which cheese is made from ewe's milk?
☐ Gorgonzola ☐ Roquefort
☐ Stilton ☐ Danish Blue

61 Where should cheese be stored?

62 Why is cheese a nutritious food?

63 The skin or rind of cheese should not show spots of m_____
as this is a sign of damp storage.

64 When cut, cheese should not give off an over-strong s_____
or any indication of a _____.

65 Name three hard, three soft and three blue vein cheeses.

1	1	1
2	2	2
3	3	3

66 Hard, semi-hard and blue vein cheese when cut should not appear

_____.

67 Soft cheese when cut should not appear r_____ but should
have a delicate c_____consistency.

68 The chief fermenting agent used in cheese making is
☐ junket ☐ plunket
☐ rennet ☐ sonnet

69 Name four English varieties of cheese.
1   3
2   4

70 Delete the odd one out in each line.
1 Cheddar, Cheshire, Camembert, Gruyère, Parmesan
2 Brie, Carré de L'Est, Demi Swiss, Gorgonzola
3 Stilton, Bel Paese, Roquefort, Danish Blue
4 Caerphilly, St Paulin, Emmental, Pont L'Eveque.

71 Name one cheese from each of the following countries.
France
Italy
Holland
Switzerland
Denmark
England

72 The hardest cheese which is produced for grating is
☐ Port Salut. ☐ Parmesan.
☐ Pommel demi-Swiss. ☐ Bel Paese.

73 The famous rich double cream cheese with blue veins made in England is

☐ Stilton ☐ Double Gloucester ☐ Dorset Blue vinny
☐ Caerphilly

74 Two of the most popular French cheeses are

☐ Camembert.
☐ St Paulin.
☐ Carré de L'Est.
☐ Brie.

75 Identify these cheeses.

1 **2** **3** **4**

13 Cereals

1 All the following cereals are used in catering. true/false?
Wheat, oats, barley, maize, rice, tapioca, sago, arrowroot.

2 All cereals contain large amounts of?

3 Flour is produced from?

4 Whole grain cereals provide vitamin

☐ A
☐ B
☐ D

5 In what atmosphere should flour be stored?

6 What is the difference between strong and soft flour?

7 Name three foods for which soft flour is suitable.
1   2   3

8 Name three foods for which strong flour is suitable.
1   2   3

9 What percentage of the whole grain is contained in
1 wholemeal flour
2 wheatmeal flour
3 white flour?

10 What is added to white flour to make it self raising?

11 What is semolina?

12 Which is the odd one out and why?
Vermicelli   Spaghetti   Macaroni   Minestroni

13 Oats have the highest food value of all the cereals. true/false?
14 The chief use of oats is
☐ gruel.   ☐ oat cakes.
☐ porridge.   ☐ Scotch broth.
15 From which cereal is cornflour obtained?
☐ wheat   ☐ oats
☐ maize   ☐ barley
16 Maize, sweetcorn, corn, corn on the cob are different names for the same food. true/false?
17 When cooked long grain rice has a _____ structure.
18 When cooked short grain rice has a _____ structure.
19 What is obtained from
1 the roots of the cassava plant? _____
2 the pith of a certain palm? _____
3 the roots of the West Indian Maranta Plant? _____
20 Why is arrowroot particular ly suitable for thickening clear sauces?

21 Arrowroot is suitable for invalids because it is easily digested. true/false?
14 **Raising agents**
1 Name three food processes in which air is used as a raising agent.
1   2   3
2 Baking powder is a chemical raising agent. true/false?
3 List five hints on using baking powder.
1
2
3
4
5
4 What is yeast?
☐ a form of plant life
☐ a chemically produced raising agent
☐ concentrated hops
☐ double strength baking powder

5 State four essential storage and quality points for fresh yeast.

6 Yeast should always be used at room temperature. true/false?

7 Yeast contains Vitamin B. true/false?

8 To enable yeast to grow which conditions are necessary?
☐ moisture, heat, salt
☐ cold liquid, sugar, proving
☐ hot liquid, salt, sugar
☐ blood heat liquid, sugar, proving

9 Does salt retard the working of yeast. yes/no?

10 Above which temperature is yeast destroyed?

☐ 12°C   ☐ 42°C
☐ 22°C   ☐ 52°C

11 Yeast can withstand low temperature without damage. true/false?

12 Why should yeast dough be well kneaded?

13 Give another word meaning kneading.

14 Proving a yeast dough means
☐ letting it rest.
☐ cutting it back.
☐ allowing it to double in size.
☐ it has satisfied the customers.

15 Name six items that are made using yeast.

1	4
2	5
3	6

16 What causes over-proving?

15 **Sugar**

1 Sugar is invaluable for producing energy. true/false?

2 Sugar is obtained from sugar b_____and sugar
c_____.

3 What percentage of pure sugar is contained in sugar?

☐ 100%   ☐ 60%
☐ 80%   ☐ 40%

4 Demerara sugar is
☐ brown sugar.   ☐ lump sugar.
☐ coffee sugar.   ☐ fine caster sugar.

5 Brown sugar is unrefined. true/false?

6 List the following in order of fineness with the finest first; icing sugar, granulated sugar and caster sugar.

1

2

3

7 What is loaf sugar?

8 Give an example of the use of each of these.

Glucose

Syrup

Treacle

16 Cocoa

1 Cocoa is a powder produced from the beans of the cacao tree. true/false?

2 Does cocoa have any food value?

3 Chocolate is produced from cocoa mass, fine sugar and cocoa butter. true/false?

4 Give three uses of chocolate couverture.

1   2   3

17 Coffee

1 Name four varieties of coffee.

1   3

2   4

2 What is the correct way to store coffee?

3 Coffee has some food value. true/false?

4 Name the methods of coffee making which apply to the illustrated equipment.

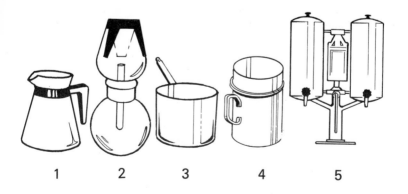

1   2   3   4   5

5 List six points to follow when making coffee.

1

2

3

4

5

6

6 How much coffee is required to produce 1 litre?

18 Tea

1 Name five tea producing countries.

1   4

2   5

3

2 Tea without sugar and/or milk has no nutritional value. true/false?

3 Why must tea be kept in airtight containers?

4 What are the five golden rules for making good tea?

1

2

3

4

5

19 Pulses

1 Pulses are the dried s_____of plants which form

p_____.

2 Name three types of pulse.

1   2   3

3 Pulses are a good source of protein. true/false?

20 Herbs

1 What value have herbs from the nutritional point of view?

☐ To provide body regulating processes.

☐ Enables starch to be converted to sugar.

☐ Creates energy from carbohydrate.

☐ Stimulates the flow of gastric juices.

2 Name five common herbs and state a suitable use for each.

1

2

3

4

5

3 Herbs may be used f_____but the majority are

d _____.

4 What is it in the leaves of herbs that gives the characteristic smell and flavour?

☐ pollen   ☐ flower buds

☐ oil   ☐ the stems

5 Which herb is a member of the onion family and has a delicate onion flavour?

6 Which is the strong pungent herb that aids the stomach to digest rich fatty meat such as pork, duck, goose?

7 What is the composition of fines-herbes?

8 Angelica is a crystallised
☐ leaf   ☐ seed   ☐ root   ☐ stem

21 Spices

1 Spices are a variety of fruits, seeds, roots, flowers or bark of different trees or shrubs. true/false?

2 Allspice is another name for mixed spice. true/false?

3 Cloves are
☐ unopened seed pods of a tree from Zanzibar.
☐ the fruit of a shrub from Penang.
☐ the flower buds of a shrub from Morocco.
☐ unopened flower buds of a tree from Madagascar.

4 Which spice is associated with the cooking of apples?

5 Which spice is the bark of the small branches of the
c_____shrub?

6 Which tropical tree bears a fruit like an apricot which when ripe has a kernel which is_____. The kernel is covered with a bright red covering which is _____.

7 Name four spices which go into mixed spice.
1   3
2   4

8 State a different use for each of these.
1 nutmeg
2 saffron
3 cinnamon
4 carraway

9 Saffron is the dried stigmas from a crocus grown chiefly in
☐ Spain   ☐ Portugal   ☐ Italy

22 Condiments

1 What causes the difference between white and black peppercorns?

2 Why is salt necessary in the diet?

3 What happens to salt if it is not kept dry?

4 From what is pepper obtained?

5 Which is the hotter - cayenne or paprika?

6 Paprika is a
- ☐ type of herb.
- ☐ oriental spice.
- ☐ mild pepper.
- ☐ kind of mustard.

7 Paprika is used in a specific dish known as _____.

8 From which country did the dish named in the previous question originate?

9 In which part of Great Britain is mustard grown?
- ☐ East Anglia
- ☐ Scilly Isles
- ☐ East Lanarkshire
- ☐ Lancashire

10 Malt vinegar is made from oats. true/false?

11 Name three types of vinegar.
1   2   3

12 Name the most expensive vinegar which has the most delicate flavour.

13 State two uses of vinegar other than preservation.
1   2

23 **Colourings, flavourings and essences**

1 What colour is cochineal?

2 Match the colours to their culinary sources.
1	green	☐ turmeric
2	red	☐ chlorophyl
3	brown	☐ cochineal
4	yellow	☐ blackjack

3 What could anchovy essence be used for?

24   **Grocery and delicatessen goods**

1   What is aspic jelly?

2   Bombay Duck is
      ☐ a small Indian duck.
      ☐ an eastern type of sweet.
      ☐ dried fillet of fish.
      ☐ a Chinese hors d'oeuvre.

3   Caviar is obtained from
      ☐ cod.   ☐ salmon.
      ☐ carp.   ☐ sturgeon.

4   The finest caviar comes from
      ☐ France, Italy, or Spain
      ☐ Russia, Persia, or Romania.
      ☐ Hungary, Yugoslavia, or Arabia.
      ☐ Holland, Belgium, or Denmark.

5   Cèpes are a
      ☐ species of French mushrooms.   ☐ kind of Italian pasta.
      ☐ type of French pancake.   ☐ variety of Italian pear.

6   What is foie gras?

7   Galantine is a
      ☐ cooked meat preparation.   ☐ kind of haggis.
      ☐ type of salami.   ☐ special vegetable dish.

8   Name the two forms in which gelatine is available and give an example
      of its use.
      1   2

9   What are gherkins?

10   Name the three main varieties of olive.
      1   M _____
      2   S _____ Q _____
      3   B _____

11   With which countries are the following associated?
      Frog's legs _____   Sauerkraut _____
      Haggis _____   Poppadum _____
      Parma ham _____   Stilton _____
      Foie gras _____   Truffles _____
      Olives _____   Escargots _____

12   Give an example of the use of
      1   capers
      2   gherkins
      3   olives

13   Walnuts are pickled after/before the shell has hardened.

14   Poppadums are
- ☐ poppy seeds.
- ☐ Indian breakfast cereal.
- ☐ an exotic oriental fruit.
- ☐ thin round biscuits.

15   Potted shrimps are preserved in
- ☐ margarine.
- ☐ oil.
- ☐ vegetable fat.
- ☐ butter.

16   Rollmops are
- ☐ curled anchovies.
- ☐ dainty bread rolls.
- ☐ rolled herring fillets.
- ☐ rolled kipper fillets.

17   Sauerkraut is made from
- ☐ white cabbage.
- ☐ green cabbage.
- ☐ red cabbage.
- ☐ a mixture of all three.

18   The ideal weight of a salmon for smoking is
- ☐ 2½ - 5   kilo
- ☐ 6   - 7½ kilo
- ☐ 10   - 11½ kilo
- ☐ 12½ - 15   kilo

19   At which course would smoked salmon be served?

20   What are escargots?

21   How would escargots be served?

22   Truffles are a f_____ and the most famous area in which they are found is the P_____ region of France.

23   A marron glacé is a peeled and cooked chestnut preserved in syrup. true/false?

24   Honey is a natural sugar produced by bees working upon the n_____of f_____.

25   Pastillage is a mixture of icing sugar and
- ☐ gum tragacanth.
- ☐ gum grysanth.
- ☐ gum organic.
- ☐ gum agnostic.

26   Rennet is used for making
- ☐ aspic.
- ☐ jelly.
- ☐ junket.
- ☐ fondant.

8   Preservation of foods

pages 258-260

1   In the air there are certain micro-organisms which cause food to go bad, called m_____, y_____, b_____.

2   When whiskers form on food they are called

3   On which three foods are whiskers likely to grow?
     1   2   3

4   Are all the micro-organisms destructive. yes/no?

5   Most micro-organisms can be checked by r_____ and killed by h_____.

6   Explain the reason for your answer to the previous question.

7   Dry foods and those containing a high percentage of sugar or vinegar are less likely to go bad. true/false?

8   Enzymes are chemical substances produced by living cells. true/false?

9   Fruits are ripened by the action of

10   When meat is hung it becomes tender due to

11   Because of enzyme activity game becomes

12   If enzyme activity goes too far foods can be spoiled. true/false?

13   To prevent enzyme activity going too far, foods must be r_____ or heated to a high t_____.

14   Which is the correct way to write the term for the degree of acidity of a food material?
     ☐ pH   ☐ HP   ☐ Ph   ☐ ph

15   What number of the range of acidity and alkaninity would you give to lemons _____ butter _____ egg white

16   The browning of cut apples and bananas is caused by enzymes. true/false?

17   What is the effect of lemon juice on cut bananas and apples?

18   Name eight ways of preserving food.
     1   5
     2   6
     3   7
     4   8

19 Drying and dehydration of food is achieved by extracting the
m _____ from the food.

20 The drying of foods prevents the growth of m_____,
y_____ and b_____.

21 Originally foods were dried in the sun. true/false?

22 What is the modern process of freezing and drying?
☐ accelerated freeze drying
☐ quick frozen drying
☐ deep frozen drying
☐ frozen and dried

23 Give three advantages of dried food
1
2
3

24 Name six foods preserved by drying.
1   4
2   5
3   6

25 Little flavour or food value is lost in the drying of food. true/false?

26 Which is the odd one out and why?
currants   sultanas   prunes   strawberries   apricots

27 Can eggs and milk be dried. yes/no?

28 Explain in a *few* words the roller and the spray processes.

29 Are micro-organisms in food killed by refrigeration. yes/no?

30 Cold storage of fresh foods retards the decay of food, it does not
prevent it from going bad. true/false?

31 Quick freezing is satisfactory because
☐ medium ice crystals are formed in the food cells.
☐ large ice crystals are formed in the food cells.
☐ small ice crystals are formed in the food cells.
☐ small ice crystals are formed outside the food cells.

32 Meat kept at a temperature just above freezing point is known as
c _____ meat.

33 The meat referred to in the previous question will keep for up to
☐ 1 month   ☐ 3 months
☐ 2 months   ☐ 6 months

34 Why are lamb carcasses frozen but not beef carcasses?

35 Both raw and cooked meats can be quick frozen. true/false?

36 State four advantages for using frozen raw foods.

    1

    2

    3

    4

37 State four advantages for using pre-cooked frozen foods.

    1

    2

    3

    4

38 What is meant by a 'blown' can?

    ☐ one that has a slight dent

    ☐ one that has no label

    ☐ one that had air blown in during processing

    ☐ one with a bulge at either end

39 What should be done with blown cans?

40 Where is the correct place to store tinned ham?

    ☐ in the deep freeze

    ☐ in the refrigerator

    ☐ in the larder

    ☐ a cool part of the kitchen

41 Tinned food will keep indefinitely. true/false?

42 List the following can sizes in order of size - largest first.

    A2   A10   14Z   A1   A2½

43 What is the advantage of preserving meat and fish by salting and smoking?

44 Name two meats preserved by salting or pickling.

    1   2

45 In what is meat pickled?

    ☐ brine

    ☐ vinegar

    ☐ vinaigrette

    ☐ spiced vinegar

46 Name four fish preserved by salting and pickling.

    1   3

    2   4

47 What is brine?

    ☐ stock containing saltpetre

    ☐ water containing iron

    ☐ a salt court bouillon

    ☐ a salt solution

48 What is the effect of adding salt to butter and margarine?

49 Name four items preserved because of the sugar content.
   1   3
   2   4

50 If too little sugar is used when making jam what will be the effect on the keeping quality?

51 Name six foods preserved in vinegar.
   1   4
   2   5
   3   6

52 Match the item with a method of preservation.
   1 Glacé   ☐ Salmon
   2 Crystallised   ☐ Peel
   3 Candied   ☐ Onions
   4 Pickled   ☐ Angelica
   5 Smoked   ☐ Sultanas
   6 Dried   ☐ Cherries

9   Storekeeping

1 A clean orderly food store run efficiently is essential in any catering establishment. true/false?

2 State three reasons for running an efficient food store.
   1
   2
   3

3 Why is it desirable for a food store to face north?

4 Why is good ventilation and freedom from dampness essential in a food store?

5 State six points necessary for a well-planned store.
   1   4
   2   5
   3   6

6 To maintain good standards of hygiene what is essential with regard to
   1 walls
   2 ceilings
   3 floors
   4 shelves?

7 All store containers should be easy to clean and have tightly fitting lids. true/false?

8 Cleaning materials, because they have a strong smell, should be kept
   ☐ on the lowest shelves in the store.
   ☐ on the highest shelves in the store.
   ☐ at one end of the store.
   ☐ in a separate store.

9 Name the two groups into which foods are divided for storage purposes.
   1   2

10 What is the correct procedure with cases of tinned food?
   ☐ leave in the cases until required
   ☐ open case at one end so that cans can easily be removed
   ☐ unpack the cases and stack on shelves
   ☐ unpack the tins, inspect them and then stack on shelves.

11 Why should dented tins be used as soon as possible?

12 Briefly describe the layout of an efficient vegetable store.

13 Name four qualities of a good storekeeper.
   1   3
   2   4

14 First in first out is a good rule for issuing stores. true/false?

15 What are requisitions?

16 Complete the headings on this incomplete bin card.

BIN CARD				
COMMODITY _	_ _ _ _ _ _ _ _ _ _	PRICE _ _ _ _ _ _ _ _ _ _ MAX. STOCK _ _ _ _ _ _ _ _ _ _ _ _ _		
	RECEIVED		STOCK IN HAND	

17 Complete the headings on this stores ledger sheet.

STORES LEDGER SHEET

Date	DETAIL		QUANTITY		UNIT	VALUE		
				Balance			Balance	Issued

18 Every time goods are received or issued the appropriate entries should be made on both the stores ledger sheet and the bin card. true/false?

19 Explain the reason for your answer to the previous question.

20 What is a departmental requisition book?

21 Complete the headings on this departmental requisition book.

DEPARTMENTAL REQUISITION BOOK						267

.... Class........................

	Quan.	Price per Unit	Issued if Different		Unit		Code	£	

22 An order book is filled in every time the storekeeper wishes to have goods delivered. true/false?

23 An order book has
☐ one copy. ☐ three copies.
☐ two copies. ☐ four copies.

24 Should all entries in the order book be signed. yes/no?

25 If you answered yes to the previous question, who should sign the orders?
☐ manager
☐ chef
☐ storekeeper
☐ finance officer

26 What is the purpose of the stock sheet?

27 Stock should be taken at regular intervals of
☐ one week or one month
☐ two weeks or two months
☐ three weeks or three months
☐ four weeks or four months

28 What is the purpose of stock-taking?

29 What is a spot check?
☐ an inspection of food to see if germs or spots are present
☐ a check of a few random items of stock
☐ a check on the cleanliness of bin cards
☐ a check on all bin card entries

30 Delivery notes are sent with goods supplied as a means of
c_____g that everything ordered has been d_____d.

31 What is the relationship between the delivery note and duplicate order sheet?

32 Invoices are sent out to clients setting out the cost of the goods supplied or services rendered. true/false?

33 Bill is another name for an

34 An invoice should be sent out
☐ on the day the goods are sent out.
☐ one month after the goods are sent out.
☐ two months after the goods are sent out.
☐ six months after the goods are sent out.

35 What do the 'terms of settlement' on a bill mean?

36 A credit note is issued stating
☐ how much is owed to the company.
☐ allowances made for adjustments and returnables.
☐ how much credit the company allows.
☐ allowances for staff meals.

37 Statements show
☐ the state of the company at the half year.
☐ details of the purchases of the quarter.
☐ summaries of invoices and credit notes for the previous month.
☐ amounts of goods returned during the month.

38 Give two examples of the use of credit notes
1   2

39 When a client makes payment he or she usually pays by cheque. Will he or she also send back the statement. yes/no?

40 Who completes the statement and where is it finally kept?

41 Cash discount is discount allowed in consideration of p _____ payment.

42 Trade discount is discount allowed by one_____to another.

43 Gross price is the price of an article before/after discount has been deducted?

44 Nett price is the price of an article before/after discount has been deducted?

45 Debit indicates the monies coming in. true/false?

46 Make entries for Monday (Out), Wednesday (In) and Thursday (Out) to agree final columns.

Daily Stores Issues Sheet

Com-modity	Unit	Stock in hand	Monday		Tuesday		Wednesday		Thursday		Friday		Total pur-chases	Total issues	Total stock
			In	Out	In	Out	In	Out	In	Out	In	Out			
Butter	kg	27												5	22
Flour	Sacks	2											1	1	2
Olive oil	Litres	8												1½	6½
Spices	30 g packs	8											8	4	12
Peas, tin	A10	30												9	21

10 Kitchen organisation and supervision

1 What points affect the organisation of the kitchen?

2 State four responsibilities of the Head Chef or Head Cook.
1
2
3
4

3 What is the French for the Second Chef?

4   A Chef de Partie is in charge of
☐ the food for small parties of customers.
☐ a section of the work in the kitchen.
☐ banquets, buffets and parties.
☐ the menus for all functions.

5   In the traditional organisation what were the responsibilities of the
1   Larder chef
2   Pastry chef
3   Sauce chef
4   Relief chef?

6   What does the word *commis* indicate?

7   Give a definition of entrées.

8   What is the name given to the chef responsible for the entrées?

9   Which partie cooks the grilled and deep fried foods?

10   What is the French name for the Fish Cook?

11   Yorkshire pudding is made by the
☐ vegetable cook   ☐ relief cook
☐ pastry cook   ☐ roast cook

12   What does the aboyeur do?
☐ act as toastmaster
☐ call out the orders
☐ carve the joints in the room
☐ look after the still room

13   Name four subsidiary departments of the kitchen
1   3
2   4

14   What are the advantages of an operation where the kitchen is on full view to the customers?

15   What effects have the continually increasing costs of space, equipment, maintenance, fuel and labour had on the organisation of the kitchen?

11   Industrial relations

pages 301-306

1   Effective relationships in industry depend upon
     1   cooperation between _____ and _____
     2   knowing _____ passed by Parliament
     3   having the _____ towards the laws.

2   List six reasons why good industrial relations are not easy to create in the catering industry.
     1
     2
     3
     4
     5
     6

3   Very briefly state the purpose of a trade union.

4   What function should the shop steward perform?

5   What should the Sex Discrimination Act prevent?

6   Who does the Race Relations Act help?

7   What is the meaning of the word 'discrimination'?

8   The Equal Pay Act specifies that equal pay is paid to whom?

9   When assessing people for employment what considerations must not affect the issue?

10   The Employment Act is concerned, among other things, with the dismissal of staff. Give two fair and two unfair grounds for dismissal.
     1
     2
     3
     4

11   What do the following initials stand for?
     AGM
     AOB

12   What is an agenda?

13   A written record of committee decisions is termed _____.

14   Why would a person be out of order?

15 Briefly explain
ex officio   status quo
quorum

16 When all present at a meeting vote for the motion it is said to be
_____.

17 A vote in favour of a motion is said to be _____.

12   Kitchen French

1 Match the following correctly:

Monday	mercredi	Thursday	jeudi
Tuesday	lundi	Friday	samedi
Wednesday	mardi	Saturday	vendredi

2 Give the French for
Begin to cook
Send up
Very carefully
Ten customers
Twice two
Floor service

3 If you were working in a kitchen in France what would you understand by
1 Faites marcher deux entrecôtes minute

2 Envoyez quatre pommes sautées

3 En vitesse

4 Arrêtez le sole grillé

4 Translate into French
January
August
Christmas

5 Translate into English
Août
la Noël
les Paques

6 Arrange in numerical order;
sept, un, dix, huit, trois, quatre, neuf, deux, six, cinq.

7 Correct the four spelling errors in the following;
Le darne de saumon
La tronçon de turbot
Le selle d'agneau
La gigot d'agneau

8 Farcir means to fry. true/false?

9 Which is correct?
☐ le homard ☐ la homard ☐ l'homard

10 Add as appropriate le, la, les.

darne	selle	goujons
tronçon	coeur	gigot

11 Tick the correct one.
☐ le fillet de sole frits ☐ les filet de sole frits
☐ la filet de sole frit ☐ les filets de sole frit

12 Correct the following.

farçi	entremetier
beure	crepes
persilees	choufleur
rôtisier	troson

13 Lemon pancakes written in French would be
☐ crépes à le citron.
☐ crêpe aux citron.
☐ crêpes au citron.
☐ crêpes au citrons.

14 Correct the four spelling errors.
Consome en tasse
Sole en gujons
Fillet de boeuf
Carrotes Vichy

15 Give the French for
Apple tart
Lobster soup
Peas French style
Mashed potatoes
Banana fritters
Ham omelet

16 What do the following mean?
1 assaisoner
2 braiser
3 chauffer
4 concasser

17 Mélanger means
☐ to mix.
☐ to muddle.
☐ to emulsify.
☐ to make.

18 Match the following.

1	au four	☐	scrambled
2	les blancs d'oeufs	☐	studded
3	au vin blanc	☐	cooked in the oven
4	brouillé	☐	a cooking liquid
5	le court bouillon	☐	mixed
6	jus rôti	☐	fixed price meal
7	napper	☐	egg whites
8	clouté	☐	gravy
9	panaché	☐	with white wine
10	table d'hôte	☐	to mask

19 Paner means
☐ to pass through a sieve.
☐ to pound.
☐ to plate.
☐ to egg and crumb.

20 A tranche-lard is
☐ a bacon slicer.
☐ a thick slice of bacon.
☐ medium chopping knife.
☐ carving knife.

21 A poche is a
☐ a pocket.   ☐ an egg poaching pan.
☐ a piping tube.   ☐ a piping bag.

22 Translate the following into French.

1	bread	3	bacon
2	butter	4	cheese

23 Translate the following into English.

1	l'oeuf	3	le jambon
2	la farine	4	le lait

24 Translate the following into French.

1	lamb	3	pork
2	beef	4	veal

25 Translate the following into English.

1	le poulet	3	la dinde
2	le canard	4	le faisan

26 Complete the French names.

Brussel sprouts	les c _____ de B _____
Cauliflower	le c _____ f _____
French beans	les h _____ v _____
Mushrooms	les c _____

27 Complete the French names.

Apple	la _____
Banana	la _____
Cherry	la _____
Lemon	le _____
Orange	l' _____
Pear	la _____
Pineapple	l' _____

28 Brunoise means
- ☐ small neat dice.
- ☐ basic brown sauce.
- ☐ braising.
- ☐ browning.

29 Contrefilet is a
- ☐ large fillet steak.
- ☐ small fillet steak.
- ☐ boned wing rib of beef.
- ☐ boned sirloin of beef.

30 Navarin is a
- ☐ navy dish of pork and beans.
- ☐ brown lamb or mutton stew.
- ☐ Normandy speciality of tripe.
- ☐ Northern France pancake.

31 Ragoût means
- ☐ grill.
- ☐ boil.
- ☐ stew.
- ☐ fried.

32 Translate this menu into French.
Watercress soup
Fried cod with tomato sauce
Chips
Apple pie

33 Which is correct?
- ☐ hors d'oeuvres variés
- ☐ hor d'oeuvre variés
- ☐ hor d'oeuvres varié
- ☐ hors d'oeuvre variés

34 Match the following.
1 la louche
2 la poche
3 la poêle
4 le lard
5 la longe
6 le chinois

- ☐ frying pan
- ☐ bacon
- ☐ loin
- ☐ ladle
- ☐ conical strainer
- ☐ piping bag

35 Which would be served as a sweet dish and which as a meat dish?
le riz
le ris

36 Translate the following into French.
cod
whitebait
haddock
oyster
prawn

37 Write the following in French suitable for the menu.

☐ stuffed loin of lamb

☐ grilled lamb chop

☐ liver and bacon

☐ braised duck with peas

☐ jugged hare

☐ cauliflower soup

☐ leaf spinach

☐ cherry tartlet

13   Menu planning

1 The aim of menu planning is to give customers what they want, not what the caterer thinks they want. true/false?

2 The traditional name given to a set menu at a set price is

☐ à la carte.

☐ chef's selection.

☐ meal of the day.

☐ table d'hôte.

3 An à la carte menu is one

☐ for customers wanting a set menu.

☐ where it is served from a buffet or cart.

☐ where the dishes are individually priced.

☐ used at a call order unit.

4 State six important points that should be taken into consideration before planning a menu.

1

2

3

4

5

6

5 Give two reasons why it is sensible to use foods in season?

1

2

6   What are the dangers of planning menus without giving consideration to the kitchen equipment available?

7   Why should the capabilities of the serving staff be considered when selecting types of dishes and plates on which food is served?

8   What is understood by menu balance?

9   Criticise the following menus.
      1   Mushroom Soup
          Fillets of Sole Bonne Femme
          Boiled Chicken and Rice
          Mushroom and Bacon Savoury.

      2   Crème Portugaise
          Fillets of Sole Dugléré
          Hungarian Goulash
          Marquise Potatoes
          Stuffed Tomatoes
          Strawberry Flan

10   State six common faults in menu planning.
      1
      2
      3
      4
      5
      6

11   What do you understand by 'plate appeal'?

12   Give two examples of plated foods to illustrate your answer to the previous question.

13 If the house policy is to write all menus in English what would you do
    with
    1   mayonnaise
    2   hors d'oeuvre
    3   consommé

14 Poulet Sauté Parmentier has a garnish of
    ☐ turned potatoes.
    ☐ duchesse potatoes.
    ☐ 1 cm dice potatoes.
    ☐ sauté potatoes.

15 Compile a four course menu illustrating good balance of texture, food
    value, colour etc.

16 Which way do you prefer to see this item on the menu?
    Give your reason why.
    ☐ Poached Turbot with Hollandaise Sauce
    ☐ Sea fresh succulent Turbot with Dutch butter sauce
    ☐ Turbot Poché Sauce Hollandaise
    ☐ Turbot Poché Sauce Hollandaise (Boiled Turbot and Hollandaise
       Sauce).

17 Match these items.
    1   Condé   ☐ Coffee
    2   Washington   ☐ Tomatoes
    3   Véronique   ☐ Sweetcorn
    4   Doria   ☐ Cucumber
    5   Mornay   ☐ Cauliflower
    6   Portugaise   ☐ Cheese
    7   Moka   ☐ Rice
    8   Dubarry   ☐ Grapes

18 Trout meunière Bretonne is shallow fried trout garnished with
    ☐ capers and lemon segments.
    ☐ turned pieces of cucumber.
    ☐ soft roes, mushrooms and tomato.
    ☐ shrimps and slices mushrooms.

19 What flavour would Suchard indicate on the menu?

20 A praliné ice cream would contain

21 In sweet dishes what ingredient is indicated by these terms?

    1   Chantilly

    2   Normande

    3   Montmorency

    4   Melba

    5   Hélène

22 What ingredient is indicated by the use of these words?

    1   Clamart

    2   Lyonnaise

    3   Florentine

    4   Princesse

23 What is the difference between a traditional English breakfast and a continental breakfast?

24 List three points to consider when compiling a breakfast menu.

    1

    2

    3

25 At which meal would these dishes most likely be served? Indicate with B for breakfast L for lunch and D for dinner.

    ☐ egg and bacon   ☐ rice pudding

    ☐ boiled beef and carrots   ☐ kipper

    ☐ treacle pudding   ☐ sorbet

    ☐ suprême de volaille   ☐ liver and bacon

26 Suggest three first courses suitable for the lunch menu in a medium priced hotel in summer.

    1

    2

    3

27 Would these dishes usually be offered for luncheon or dinner?

    braised oxtail   braised sweetbreads

    steak and kidney pudding   Irish stew

    chicken casserole   hot pot

28 Suggest three light traditional English sweets suitable for a worker's canteen menu in summer.

    1   2   3

29 Suggest a typical three course English luncheon menu for a party of overseas visitors on their first visit to England.

30 The party in the previous question who had an early breakfast and a light lunch, require a real English tea. What would you offer them?

31 Suggest eight suitable items for a dish of French pastries.

1	5
2	6
3	7
4	8

32 Name four popular items that may be served toasted for tea.

| 1 | 3 |
| 2 | 4 |

33 Suggest three interesting first courses for dinner at a commercial hotel in winter.

1   2   3

34 Indicate the fish which are more suitable for dinner menus than lunch menus?

☐ cod   ☐ sole
☐ herring   ☐ salmon-trout

35 A sorbet is a

☐ type of sauce.   ☐ lightly frozen water ice.
☐ type of vegetable.   ☐ a double sized sausage.

36 Suggest three interesting sweets suitable for hospital patients on a normal diet in winter.

1   2   3

37 Suggest a four course dinner menu for 24 very important people to be served in November with no expense spared.

38 In April the office block annual party for 100 people require a light supper at 11 pm. What would you offer them?

39   Match these items.

1 Entrée   ☐ Macaroni au gratin
2 Roast   ☐ Vol-au-vent
3 Savoury   ☐ Egg mayonnaise
4 Farinaceous   ☐ Welsh rarebit
5 Hors d'oeuvre ☐ Best end of lamb

40   On which courses of the menu would these dishes be placed?
Cheese soufflé
Raised pie
Whitebait
Camembert
Potted shrimps

41   State two important points to be considered when compiling a banquet menu.
1
2

42   Why would heavily garnished dishes be avoided for banquets?

43   Can banquets be offered for both luncheon and dinner. yes/no?

44   Name four different types of buffet.
1   3
2   4

45   Suggest a menu for one of the buffets named in the previous answer, for 250 people at Christmas in a moderately priced seaside hotel.

46   What is an essential requirement for food prepared for a fork buffet?

47   It is usual to serve canapés as one of the varieties of foods at cocktail parties. true/false?

48   Suggest six interesting canapés.
1   4
2   5
3   6

49   What size should canapés be?

50   Name six items of a savoury nature suitable for a buffet.
1   4
2   5
3   6

14   Buying, costing and control

pages 375-378

1 For purchasing commodities a s_____ k_____ of all commodities is essential.

2 Which guide to purchasing should be followed?
☐ the cheapest is the best
☐ compare quality with price
☐ the dearest is always the best
☐ the best quality is the cheapest

3 List ten points which assist in the efficient buying of food.

1	6
2	7
3	8
4	9
5	10

4 Out-of-date price lists should be consulted. true/false?

5 What do you understand by portion control?

6 Why should portion control be linked closely with the buying of food?

7 Better quality food usually gives a better yield than inferior quality food. true/false?

8 The golden rule to use when considering portion control is a f_____ p_____ for a f_____ p_____.

9 Indicate which points should be considered regarding portion control.
☐ the type of customer or establishment
☐ the Safety at Work Act
☐ the quality of the food
☐ the qualifications of the kitchen staff
☐ the buying price of the food
☐ the gas and electricity services available

10 Name six items of equipment that assist portion control.

1	3	5
2	4	6

11 Approximately how many portions of soup would be obtained from a litre?
☐ 1-2
☐ 3-4
☐ 4-6
☐ 7-8

12 Approximately how many portions of haddock would be obtained from 1kg of haddock fillet?
☐ 2
☐ 4
☐ 6
☐ 8

13 Approximately how many portions would be obtained from 1 litre of custard?
☐ 16-24
☐ 25-30
☐ 32-36
☐ 40-50

14 Sausages are obtainable 12, 16, or 20 to the kg. true/false?

15 Approximately how many portions would be obtained from 1kg unpeeled old potatoes?
☐ 2- 3
☐ 4- 6
☐ 7- 8
☐ 9-10

16 How many sheep's kidney's would be a portion?
☐ 1   ☐ 2   ☐ 3   ☐ 4

17 What are the advantages of an efficient costing system?

18 One costing system will suit any type of catering establishment. true/false?

19 What are the three main elements that make up the total cost of an item or a meal?
1   F_____ or m_____ cost
2   L_____
3   O_____

20 Food and materials are known as _____ costs.
Labour and overheads are known as _____ costs.

21 List six examples of item 3 in the previous question.
1   4
2   5
3   6

22 Gross profit or kitchen profit is the difference between the
c_____ of the food and the s_____ p
_____ of the food.

23 Net profit is the difference between the s _____ p
_____ of the food (s   ) and the total cost.

24 Sales minus food cost =
Sales minus total cost =
Food cost plus gross profit =

25 Profit is expressed as a percentage of the _____ price.

26 Finding the food costs helps control costs, prices and profits.
true/false?

27 Will an efficient food cost system help prevent waste and stealing.
yes/no?

28 Sales less food cost =
☐ gross profit
☐ net profit
☐ gross price
☐ net price

29 In the metric system what do these refer to?
SI
g
m
ml

30 The caterer who gives the customer value for money together with the
type of food the customer wants is well on the way to being successful.
true/false?

15 The computer in catering

1 What are the small plastic squares containing layers of minute circuits
pressed together called?
☐ data   ☐ floppy discs
☐ chips   ☐ programs

2 What type of routine _____ job can be done with the
application of computer technology?

3 What is the name given to information stored by the computer?
☐ dictum   ☐ datum
☐ datsun   ☐ data

4 What is the name given to information processed by the computer?

5 What is the name given to the manufactured equipment we know as a
computer?
☐ hardstore   ☐ hardware
☐ hardstock   ☐ hardstack

6 Instructions to computers are on tapes which are known as software.
true/false?

7   The television screen with a keyboard like a typewriter is often the most distinctive feature of the computer and is known as a VDU. What do the letters stand for?

8   An important part of the printer is the daisy wheel. What is the function of the daisy wheel?

9   What is meant by a recipe explosion?

10   Which is the smaller the minicomputer or the microcomputer?

Humorous questions

1   Would melted butter be served with silver fish?

2   On being told to draw the chicken would you use pen or pencil?

3   Would fans in the kitchen be Chelsea or Manchester United supporters?

4   Is a U bend a road sign in the kitchen?

5   Which garden would Basil and Rosemary have time to go and meet the sage in?

6   Would John Dory be suitable as the fish cook?

7   Is a salamander kept in the kitchen to catch insects?

8   Would you expect the governor to be in the chef's office?

9 If ox tongues are to be found in the larder, where would you find cats' tongues?

10 Sausage meat is rolled in puff pastry, what is rolled in a blanket?

11 Would you expect chillies to feel the cold?

12 Why might the skate want to fly?

13 When stock-taking would the storekeeper take fish stock or brown stock?

14 Is it true that the still room at breakfast time is a peaceful place?

15 Which chef de partie has most cause to grumble after 12th August?

16 Could a culinary symphony be composed using triangles, mandolins, pipes, drums and horns?

17 If you were 'knocking it back' in the pastry would you be having a pint?

18 Would China or Indian tea be made with water from the fish kettle?

19 Could you end up in court with the copper?

20 Would you expect to find a seal in or under the sink?

Answers on Page 93.

General questions

Trade Descriptions Act (page 330)
1   The Trade Descriptions Act is concerned with
     ☐ a clear account of the trade practised.
     ☐ an accurate description of the item offered for sale.
     ☐ a description of the various jobs in the trade.
     ☐ an accurate account of the trades union.

2   If it was stated on the menu 'eggs and bacon', should one, or more than one egg be served?

3   It would be a contravention of the Trade Descriptions Act to write on the menu fillet of haddock and serve fillet of cod. true/false?

Preservation of food (pages 155, 267)
1   Name a substitute for wheat flour for use in thickening foods to be deep-frozen.

2   the nutritional value of foods such as texturised vegetable protein should be
     ☐ not more than the natural food it simulates.
     ☐ less than the natural food it simulates.
     ☐ considerably less than the natural food it simulates.
     ☐ equal to the natural food it simulates.

Work study (pages 17-21)
1   A skilled craftsman achieves a high standard of work with the
     ☐ least effort.
     ☐ most effort.
     ☐ great effort.
     ☐ considerable effort.
2   State three savings that can be made to reduce wastage by studying working methods.
3   In addition to paying attention to good working habits it is desirable to
     ☐ cultivate the right attitude to work.
     ☐ to take 'short cuts' and finish early.
     ☐ to work as fast as possible, irrespective of result.
     ☐ to adopt an attitude of not accepting advice.

Organisation (pages 282-286)

1 State four reasons why catering has developed in this country.

    1   3

    2   4

2 Name two people who did much to create high standards in the hotel industry before World War II.

    1   2

3 The variety and number of dishes on the menu does not affect the organisation of the kitchen. true/false?

4 Give three examples of situations where large numbers of people need to be served food at the same time.

    1

    2

    3

5 State a major advantage of the cook-freeze system.

Kitchen supervision (pages 293-300)

1 Good supervision is the effective us of

    1 m_____ 2 m_____ 3_____

2 State the three functions of a supervisor.

3 A supervisor needs to be able t_____ d_____ as well as knowing h_____ t_____ d_____.

4 Give an example of why a supervisor needs to forecast and plan.

5 Complete the following.

Organising consists of ensuring that w_____is wanted, is w_____ it is wanted, w_____ it is wanted in the r_____ amount at the r_____ time.

6 Delegation is an important aspect of supervision. true/false?

7 A good supervisor

    ☐ creates problems.

    ☐ makes problems.

    ☐ anticipates problems.

    ☐ causes problems.

8 Tick those qualities which an effective supervisor needs.
  ☐ good communicator
  ☐ tactless
  ☐ impetuous
  ☐ possess technical knowledge
  ☐ organising ability
  ☐ understanding of people
  ☐ motivator
  ☐ disciplinarian

9 An example of social influence on the catering industry would be

10 Tick the following items which could be described as having an economic effect on the catering industry.
  ☐ unemployment   ☐ a very wet summer
  ☐ rail strike   ☐ a decrease in VAT

Answers to humorous questions

1   Not likely! Silver fish are very small insects found in very damp places.
2   Neither, you would take out the chicken innards.
3   More likely extractor fans for ventilation. Some of the staff could be supporters of these clubs.
4   No, it is a bend in the pipe under the sink.
5   The herb garden − Basil, Rosemary, Thyme (pronounced 'time') and Sage are all herbs.
6   He could be, but John Dory is the name of a fish with thumb marks.
7   Most unlikely, lizards are not kept in kitchens. This salamander is for grilling foods.
8   You might, but a governor is fitted to most gas catering appliances.
9   In the pastry. Langues de chats (cats' tongues) are a type of biscuit.
10 Any person unlucky enough to have their clothing on fire.
11 Not really since they are a type of mildly hot pepper.
12 Because it's got wings!
13 Neither, he would take a list of the contents of the store.
14 No, because it's not still then, it's the still room's busiest time.
15 The roast cook, because grouse are now in season.
16 Maybe. Triangles are used as pot stands, mandolins for slicing, pipes for piping, drums for salt and horns for cream horns.
17 More likely to be kneading or working the yeast dough.
18 Neither. Fish only are cooked in fish kettles.
19 Only if you stole it! You are likely to use the copper on the stove.
20 Under the sink. It's the water in the U bend which forms a seal.

Answers to diagram questions

p. 8 q. 35   Air

p. 9 q. 41   A

p. 10 q. 8   Hair long and uncovered − scratching hair over food thus risking possibility of dandruff or/and loose hair falling into food

p. 11 q. 15   Mouth, nostrils, ears

p. 12 q. 20   Apron too short, sleeves rolled up, high-heeled shoes, wearing watch and ring, hair too long and not protected

p. 13 q. 25   Long unprotected hair and smoking over food

p. 15 q. 52   Pork pie and trifle

p. 16 q. 65   Chicken being drawn on same board as cooked meat being sliced − risk of infection

p. 16 q. 69   Salmonella

p. 17 q. 78   Bird's nest, rats, swill uncovered, flies, fish and bread on same table, W.C. door open to kitchen

p. 19 q. 1   A Conduction   B Radiation   C Convection

p. 20 q. 6   8612

p. 22 q. 6   1 Supply pipe   2 Overflow pipe   3 Ball and lever arm 4 Correct water level   5 Standpipe   6 Bell tap   7 Ball 8 Flushing pipe

p. 24 q. 15   1 Deep fat fryer   2 High pressure steamer   3 Bratt pan   4 Boiler pan   5 Steamer

p. 27 q. 43   1 Braising pan   2 Sauté pan   3 Sauteuse   4 Salmon kettle

p. 28 q. 55   Friture − iron, Conical strainer − tinned steel, Mushroom − wood, Sugar boiler − copper

p. 30 q. 21   Onion

p. 30 q. 28   Blackcurrants, because they do not contain fat

p. 32 q. 43   Oily fish because it is the only food containing Vitamin D

p. 39 q. 35   No 2

p. 44 q. 26   A Brill   B Turbot

p. 45 q. 46   A Crab   B Lobster   C Prawn   D Shrimp   E Scallop

p. 46 q. 48   A Crayfish   B Crawfish

p. 50 q. 50   A Pear − William, Comice, Conference

B Apple – Worcester pearmain, Cox's orange pippin, Bramley

C Melon – Honeydew, Canteloupe, Charentais

p. 51 q. 58 1 Walnut 2 Brazil 3 Almond 4 Coconut
5 Chestnut

p. 56 q. 75 1 Edam 2 Camembert 3 Brie 4 Gruyère

p. 59 q. 4 1 Jug 2 Cona 3 Saucepan 4 Expresso 5 Still set

p. 69 q. 16 Unit Min. Stock

p. 70 q. 17 Invoice or Reg. No. Received Issued Received

p. 70 q. 21 Date Description Unit Quan. Price per Unit

p. 72 q. 46

	Monday Out	Wed In	Thurs Out
Butter	2	0	3
Flour	1	1	0
Olive Oil	1	0	$\frac{1}{2}$
Spices	4	8	0
Peas	6	0	3